THE PHOTOSHOP AND PAINTER ARTIST TABLET BOOK

Creative Techniques in Digital Painting

Cher Threinen-Pendarvis

Peachpit Press

The Photoshop and Painter Artist Tablet Book

Cher Threinen-Pendarvis
http://www.pendarvis-studios.com

Peachpit Press
1249 Eighth Street
Berkeley, CA 94710
(510) 524-2178
(800) 283-9444
(510) 524-2221 (fax)
Find us on the World Wide Web at: http://www.peachpit.com
To report errors, please send a note to errata@peachpit.com

Peachpit Press is a division of Pearson Education.

Peachpit Press Editors: Jennifer Eberhardt, Karyn Johnson, Cary Norsworthy
Cover design: Mimi Heft
Cover illustration: Cher Threinen-Pendarvis
Book design, art direction and layout: Cher Threinen-Pendarvis
Technical Editor: Elizabeth Meyer
Copyeditor: Karen Gill
Proofreader: Jessica McCarty
Indexer: Joy Dean Lee
Production and prepress manager: Jonathan Parker

This book was set using the Minion and Helvetica families. It was written and composed in Adobe PageMaker 6.52. Final output was computer to plate at Courier Kendallville, Kendallville, Indiana.

ISBN 0-321-16891-7

0 9 8 7 6 5
Printed and bound in the United States of America.

To our Creator,
from whom all inspiration comes.
To my husband Steven,
for his friendship and love.
To my mother, Wanda, and my father, Claude.
— Cher Threinen-Pendarvis

Acknowledgments

The Photoshop and Painter Artist Tablet Book would not have been possible without a great deal of help from some extraordinary people and sources. This book has been in progress for more than two years—during that time I wrote two editions of *The Painter Wow! Book*—and it's been a wonderful journey along the way.

Heartfelt thanks go to my special friend and colleague Linnea Dayton who brainstormed with me during the early book development process. My warmest thanks also go to my longtime artist friend Bert Monroy, for writing such a wonderful foreword for the book.

A special thank you goes to the talented designer John Odam, for his inspiration and friendship. John designed the clever sidebar icons and also gave helpful critiques of the early book cover designs. Warm thanks go to my photographer friend Melinda Holden for her beautiful photographs of my studio, location painting, and work process.

I'd like to thank my co-workers "behind the scenes" on *The Photoshop and Painter Artist Tablet Book* team. I'm grateful to Elizabeth Meyer and Don Jolley for their helpful technical reads. Warmest thanks go to Karen Gill for her helpful copy editing; Jessica McCarty for her detailed proofreading; Joy Dean Lee for her careful indexing; and production manager Jonathan Parker for his thorough production and prepress expertise.

Sincere thanks go to my friends at Peachpit Press. The inspiration for this book came to me several years ago. A special thank you goes to Nancy Ruenzel for understanding my vision and for her support of the book. My warmest thanks go to Cary Norsworthy for her advice in the early stages of the book; to Jennifer Eberhardt, who gave me wonderful editing feedback through the development of the project; to Karyn Johnson, who cheerfully offered her editing help during the later phases of the book; and to the rest of the publishing team for their support. Thank you, Peachpit, for giving me the opportunity to write this book.

A special thank you goes to Ted Nace and Linnea Dayton for giving me the opportunity to publish my first book, *The Painter Wow! Book*.

A big thank you goes to the wonderful folks at Wacom for their incredible pressure-sensitive tablets that help us artists unlock the creative power of Painter and Photoshop. My special thanks go to Mark Mehall and Scott Rawlings for their support of this book, and to Burton Holmes, Will Reeb, and Kelly Ann Schroeder for their help. A warm thank you also goes to the Wacom folks that I've enjoyed working alongside at the trade shows and conferences—Peter Deitrich, Rich Harris, Weston Maggio, and the rest of the Wacom team.

My warmest thanks go to the brilliant creators of Painter—Mark Zimmer, Tom Hedges and John Derry—for creating such an incredible program.

My sincere thank you goes to Rick Champagne and Sean Young, the Program Manager and Product Manager for Painter, and to Jessica Gould, the Senior Communications Manager, for their support. I'm also grateful to the Painter development team: Christopher Tremblay, Vladmir Makarov, Max Kuzmin, Dan Jette, Valentin Ivanov, Philippe Casgrain, and to the QA folks—Kerry Liberty and Tom Watts. A warm thank you also goes to Wes Pack, the Painter graphics evangelist who I have enjoyed working with at conferences.

My special thanks go to the great people at Adobe—Tom and John Knoll, Mark Hamburg, Chris Cox and to Jerry Harris (PixelPaint co-creator and creator of the Brush engine in Photoshop 7), and the rest of the team for creating such an awesome program. My warmest thanks go to the people at Adobe who were supportive of this book—especially John Nack and Gwyn Weisberg.

My sincere thank you goes to Dan Steinhardt and all of the folks at Epson for their scanner and color printers that were helpful for testing printmaking techniques.

Thank you to all of our inspiring artist friends, colleagues and family: Judy and Douglas Atwater; Carol Benioff; John Belik; Drew and Susannah Bandish; Ken and Stephanie Goldman; Robert and Barbara Goldman; Mary, Bob and Brittany Envall; Rick Geist; Glenn Hening; Michele Jacquin and Jim; Jane Magee; Janine, Len, Tyler and Max Packett; Mike, Story, Mikayla and Kenzie McDonald; Annie Wynhausen; Mark Snovell; Thomas Threinen and family; Linnea and Paul Dayton; Jack and Jill Davis; Bert Monroy and Zosia; Sharon Steuer and Jeff; Mark and Mary Zimmer; John, Pam, and Logan Derry; Chelsea Sammel and Peter; Kathy Hamon; Claude Szwimer; Jean-Luc Touillon; Lynda Weinman, Bruce, and Jaimie; Tanya Staples and Matt; Rick and Alice Champagne, Katrin Eismann and John; Pedro Meyer; Renata and Mario Spiazzi; Mike, Pam, April and Kai Casey; the boys at Diamond Glassing; and other friends and family. I love you all.

My sincere thank you goes to my inspiring art professors, Professor Daryl Groover, Dr. Paul Lingren and Dr. Jean Swiggett. Thank you for encouraging my work.

A warm thank you goes to our Pendarvis family for their support and love, Poppa Les, Momma Anne, Larry and Joy; Patrice, David, Matt and Dylan Goodale; Michael, Liz, Paige and Bryn; Jon and Kelly; Jeremy, Michelle, Brooke and Brady Young; and Heather and Manny Faria.

A special thank you goes to our nephew Brady and niece Brooke who loaned me their colorful wooden trains so that I could use them for reference when painting *The Three Trains* illustration for Chapter 9. A special thank you goes to our nieces Paige and Bryn whose colorful artwork decorates our kitchen and brings us smiles. A warm acknowledgment goes to Jenna Klein and Armand Barolotti, two very talented young friends. You have a wonderful creative life ahead of you.

A heartfelt thank you to these special "coworkers:" to my husband Steve, for his encouragement and patience; and to our cats Soshi, Pearl, Sable and Marika, the close companions who keep me company in the studio. (Marika provided me with (sometimes) welcome interruptions that caused me to take breaks, by volleying her toy mouse onto my computer keyboard so we could play fetch.) Warm thanks go to my sister-in-law Joy Young and dear friends Lisa Baker, Susan Bugbee, Skip Frye, Don Jolley, Julie Klein, and Elizabeth Meyer who shared sincere encouragement and prayers. Thanks for checking in with me while I worked, and for the fun lunch breaks that we shared in the water at our favorite surf spot.

Finally, I would like to thank all the other family, friends, and colleagues who have been so patient and understanding during the development of this book.

About the Author and Artist

Hand-working a digital print of Path to Water, North *using soft pastel*

An award-winning artist and author, Cher Threinen-Pendarvis has always worked with traditional art tools. A native Californian, her artwork is a reflection of the inspiring travels she made with her family around the Pacific Rim—Hawaii, the Philippines, Japan, and China, to name a few. Her mother Wanda was also an artist and their times of sitting together and drawing on location was especially inspiring to Cher as she developed her interest in plein-air painting. Painting on location has also brought her closer to her community in San Diego, where she has lived most of her life, because of her volunteer efforts to help protect the Sunset Cliffs Natural Park—a place she often paints.

A pioneer in digital art, Cher has created illustrations using the Macintosh computer for nearly two decades. (Some of her early drawings with a mouse can be seen in the gallery at the back of the book.) She has been widely recognized for her mastery of Painter, Photoshop and the

Borrego, *a traditional watercolor painted in plein air on Arches cold-pressed watercolor paper*

Agaves on the Edge, Summer, *painted using the Artists' Oils medium in Painter IX using location sketches for reference*

Wacom pressure-sensitive tablet, and has used these electronic tools since they were first released. Exercising her passion for Painter's artist tools, Cher has worked as a consultant and demo-artist for the developers of Painter. Her artwork has been exhibited worldwide and her articles and art have been published in many books and periodicals. Cher holds a BFA with Highest Honors and Distinction in Art specializing in painting and printmaking, and she is a member of the San Diego Museum of Art Artist Guild and the Digital Art Guild.

She has taught Painter and Photoshop workshops around the world, and is principal of the consulting firm Cher Threinen Design. Cher is author of all seven editions of *The Painter Wow! Book*. The upcoming *Painter IX Wow! Book* is the latest edition of this highly-praised volume of techniques and inspiration.

To learn more about Cher, please visit her Web site at www.pendarvis-studios.com. To learn more about the book, please visit the support Web site for the book at www.peachpit.com/tabletbook.

Foreword

Why should this book go hand in hand with the purchase of a computer and graphics software? What makes this book so important?

There is a creative side that we all possess. The computer has opened up enormous opportunities with new tools that once we could only dream about. Whether we're creating music or video, or a music video, every sudden impulse can become a reality. For the painter or illustrator, the toolbox is almost endless. The creative process flows unabated as you switch between tools and colors with a click. Every tool, from the finest paintbrush to a piece of chalk, is there in an instant. Technology, like the Wacom pressure-sensitive tablet, has reached a point where the very tool that is held by the hand to interact with the computer looks and feels like a pen. However, with these tools there comes a learning curve. This book shortens that learning curve significantly.

Cher Threinen-Pendarvis is a digital artist who I have had the pleasure of calling my friend for many years; I met her not long after I entered the digital art realm. I have seen her talent and vision evolve through many years of dedication and exploration of graphics software and digital tools.

Companies that produce graphics software call upon her to demonstrate the features of their products. Her vast experience, coupled with her amazing talent for teaching, has produced a book that can be of tremendous help when trying to master digital tools. The many illustrations throughout the book clearly demonstrate the point being made and are beautiful. Looking at the book, I would say it's great just to have in your collection.

Now, let me tell you why this book is so important.

I have been involved in the digital art world for over two decades. In that time I have seen many changes in the way digital art is perceived. I like to compare digital art to photography when it comes to the art world's acceptance of the digital medium as an art form.

When photography became widespread, it was not considered an art form because the belief was that "anyone could take a picture." It wasn't long before we realized that it took something more to produce an Ansel Adams. Sure, anyone could take a picture but one that was worth looking at required a little thing called talent.

A similar misconception hampers computer-generated art from being fully accepted as an art form. "The computer does all the work" is a phrase I have often heard. Funny how ridiculous that statement becomes when you sit in front of a blank canvas in Photoshop or Painter and wait for something to happen.

To illustrate the point, many years ago I was conducting a class called Advanced Illustration on Computers. One of the class assignments was to create an image from life. I assigned the task of illustrating the very computer the students were working on. One young lady was having a very difficult time with the assignment. It was obvious she could not draw. I asked what she did at the company that was paying for her class and she told me she was a clerk. When asked why the company had sent her to such a class, the response sent a shiver up my spine. "They want me to learn the Mac so when I return they can fire the art director and have me do his job." Hmmmm, learn the computer and you become an instant artist. Seems we've made that mistake before.

A computer, in one way or another, touches every facet of our daily lives. Most households today have a computer. Usually it is used to fulfill the basic functions of today's technology-driven society: email, access to the Internet, work, and games. The computer, however, also puts at your disposal the tools that allow you to be creative.

Many artistic endeavors require that you buy numerous tools and materials that are specific to that craft. If you are a digital artist, however, it's possible that you've never even thought of going out and buying a set of watercolor paints and brushes. You might never have considered stretching canvas and picking out a good easel. Chances are, however, if you bought a scanner, those tools came bundled with it. Better yet, you made the commitment and bought full versions of Photoshop and Painter. Suddenly you have at your disposal all the tools necessary to create artistic masterpieces if you so desire. The condition, of course, is the talent factor.

Many do have a talent but never had any training. Others don't have great talent but enjoy playing. In either case, a little education can make a vast difference in the end result. That's where this book comes in.

Cher comes from a traditional background with training in the fundamentals of art. Composition and shading are terms that rarely enter the vocabulary of the average person, yet are so vital to the creation of a piece of artwork—these are the subjects she lives with.

What she is doing with this book is filling in those educational gaps that the average computer user is hampered by. Cher is an educator. If you have ever attended any of her seminars or heard her speak at a trade show, you know how eloquently she can dispense information. She has a soothing voice yet it conveys the excitement she feels about the digital medium. Somehow she has managed to transfer the patience and understanding she demonstrates as a teacher onto the words in this book.

As an expert in both Photoshop and Painter, Cher shows you the processes for effects from within either program or a combination of the two. She guides you through the nuances achieved by the use of pressure-sensitive tablets. Then she teaches you how to take your concepts beyond the obvious—to that realm where creativity takes on a life of its own.

As I mentioned earlier, there are bountiful illustrations throughout the book that take you clearly through the processes she is explaining. This book is the art class you never took and wish you had. It might not make you a Michelangelo but it will give you an understanding of the basics of art. It will give you the confidence to take your doodles to the next level.

Photoshop and Painter are complex pieces of software but Cher brings them down to a manageable level so you can use them to let your creative juices run wild.

I have no doubt you will refer to this book over and over again.

Bert Monroy
Berkeley, California, October 2004

Contents

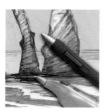

Introduction

Early artists used charcoal from their cooking fires to decorate the walls of their cave homes. Inspired by a cave painting I saw in the Dordogne valley in France, I drew this sketch using an Intuos tablet and Charcoal brushes in Painter.

I was inspired to write this book because I have enjoyed using digital art tools for nearly two decades, and I am amazed by how the tools have matured and become more sensitive and user-friendly. One of the main inspirations for the book comes from the new form of creativity that the tablet and stylus give to artists. Without them, we could not enjoy painting sensitive brushwork in Photoshop and Painter—two programs that are continuously maturing with each release. Although this book has been written for those readers using Painter IX and Photoshop CS and earlier versions, the lessons are all presented in a way that can be applied to future releases of the software.

Who This Book Is For. I have written this book for artists, illustrators, photographers, and designers of all levels who want to tap the creative power of using a tablet with Photoshop and Painter and develop their own style of painting with these applications. Whether you are an experienced artist or are just beginning to dabble and are nervous about your artistic skills, the computer can help you reach new freedom and confidence. If you are an experienced artist, you can paint from life using the eye-to-hand coordination that you developed as an artist. If you don't feel confident drawing from scratch, this book offers exercises that will give you practice. Painting using a computer is more

forgiving than most conventional media because you can draw or assemble a composition and save multiple versions as you work. You can try new approaches to your composition, undo without ruining your work, and open a previously saved version and begin again from that point. So much is possible with the computer.

Drawing using a good quality tablet and cordless stylus is completely free and natural whether you draw from life, from memory, or use a reference. The art tools and hardware have become so good in recent years that you can work with the new tools and become immersed in the creative process in much the same way that you can using traditional tools.

Conch Shell *shows the sensitive shading that is possible using an Intuos tablet and Chalk presets in Photoshop*

Using custom oil brushes and texture-sensitive chalk brushes in Painter, I painted Distribudor, *shown here as a detail.*

The Artist's Digital Tools. Painter, Photoshop, and the stylus and tablet are new "mark-making" tools in a long ancestral line of art tools. Early artists drew scenes of their daily life on the walls of their cave homes using charcoal from their cooking fires and paint made from clay and

 Drawn by hand. To keep your hand-to-eye coordination in practice, it's a good idea to keep a sketchbook with you at all times. This is also useful for recording details that inspire you, and for making notes. You might also enjoy using your laptop, tablet, and pen for sketching. In Chapter 1 you'll find information about setting up for drawing on location.

natural tints on the surfaces of stones. Later, many kinds of wet paint media (such as oil-based paint) and dry media (such as pencils and pastels) were invented. With the invention of photography, artists were able to develop a keener eye as they captured their visions with a camera. And for centuries, artists have found printmaking processes like etching and intaglio to be important for their craft.

Today, think of your stylus and the brushes in Painter and Photoshop as a new kind of pencil, a new kind of charcoal, a new kind of watercolor paint, a new oil paint, and more!

Photoshop is an essential tool for illustrators and artists who want to do retouching, compositing, color

correction, painting, and more. If you draw and paint, Painter is an essential tool because of the realism of its natural media brushes, textures, its unique special effects, and the tactile feel of its paint media. The

 Digital to conventional. A study painted on the computer can also be used as a reference for artwork done with conventional tools. My husband Steve is a surfboard builder. We often draw studies on the computer, make large prints, and then use them as references when painting on surfboards using acrylic paint. I have also used my digital studies as references for traditional art on paper or canvas, painted using conventional media.

Detail of Sunrise, *painted in Photoshop, features brushwork that enhances the center of interest*

portability between the two programs has become very good and they complement one another well. The tablet and stylus are really the bridge between your expressive hand and the computer. They give you the freedom to produce pressure-sensitive brushwork in Painter and Photoshop. When used together, all of these tools are capable of making your artwork reflect your creative intent.

Approach. This book is not a replacement for the documentation that ships with the tablet, Photoshop, or Painter, and it doesn't cover every function of these products. Instead, it focuses on features related to drawing and painting using a stylus such as: assembling brushes and paint; choosing brushes that change their brushstroke shape, opacity, or texture based on hand movement; and customizing brushes to work better with a tablet and pen.

The Photoshop and Painter Artist Tablet Book covers composition, line, tone and form, enhancing the focal point, simulating canvas and paper, mixing media, and more. In the early chapters of this book you'll have an opportunity to express yourself using different approaches to drawing (such as contour and gesture) using your stylus and tablet with Painter and Photoshop. Following the exercises on linear drawing, you'll find projects that will give you practice with modeling form, using

Using photography creatively with painting. Artists such as Leonardo da Vinci and Jan Vermeer were known to use the camera obscura and other similar devices to help them sketch out proportions quickly in their compositions. In the nineteenth century, Eugene Delacroix, Edgar Degas, Thomas Eakins, and others used the camera as a reference source. Contemporary artists have used the technique of projecting a slide on their canvas as they lay out their compositions.

A photograph can be an aid and an inspiration, but try not to fall into the practice of copying the entire photograph. Instead, I suggest pulling elements from the photograph that you want in your composition. To create a great image you need to carefully study your subject and pay attention to elements such as highlight and shadow, form, and modeling. In Chapters 9, 13, and 14, I'll show you how to use a photo for reference and to incorporate several elements into a composition.

If you are a photographer who wants to add brushwork to your images, the exercises in Chapters 4–7 will be helpful to you. These chapters will help you practice good methods of visualizing your subject and hand-to-eye coordination, and your ability to render line and form will improve. As you work, you'll gain practice in how to see the forms and how to paint brushstrokes that will reveal the forms. If you want to paint over your photos, you'll learn techniques for thinking about your subject and its forms and modeling them. This experience will be evident in your work.

value and tone. Then you'll discover projects that will help you improve your compositions, for instance, by enhancing the focal point in a painting, by simulating canvas and paper, using mixed media, composing an image from your imagination, and more.

The projects in the book are presented with color illustrations that are my own creations. You may pre-fer different subject matter or work in a different style, but these illustrations are intended to show you how to apply the techniques to use in your own work. I hope you enjoy the artwork, creative thought processes, and techniques in this book.

 Record the light of the moment. Because light changes so quickly when you're painting on location, you can record the light as it was at that moment by shooting a digital photo and then use the photo as a reference to help remember the lighting in your scene when you get back to your studio. However, in my opinion, the digital photo will not replace the experience of creating elements for your painting on location. I recommend taking the time to at least do a composition drawing and make color notes while on location.

Color and value. Will your colored painting hold up in black and white? When I painted this pastel painting in color, I massed the darker shapes together toward the right side and in the foreground as part of the composition design. To make sure I achieved a full range of tones—from the darkest values in the shadows to accents of white in the highlights—I squinted my eyes to blur the image, visually reducing it to dark and light shapes. Then I added deeper values and brighter highlights where needed. Notice how the composition holds up when converted to black and white.

Path to Water, North *was begun on location (using a laptop, Wacom tablet and Painter) at Sunset Cliffs Natural Park in San Diego, California. It was painted with the Pastel and Chalk brushes in Painter.*

How to Use This Book

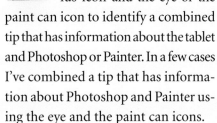

An overview and artist statement are located facing the featured art on the opening spreads.

So that you can read through the development of an art project without getting bogged down with too many technical details, I designed *The Photoshop and Painter Artist Tablet Book* using a modular approach. Each chapter includes an overview, a statement about the chapter, an Artist's Materials sidebar for each project, artist information sidebars, tablet and stylus sidebars, Photoshop sidebars, and Painter sidebar elements.

 Each chapter begins with a chapter overview of what you'll learn in the chapter. The chapter overview is followed by an artist statement about the drawing or painting projects. The artist statement is identified by an artist palette. Throughout the chapters you'll also find more artist statements and tips identified by the artist palette.

After the overview, page at the beginning of each project, you'll find an Artist's Materials box that contains the tools that you'll use in the project. Right above the Artist's Materials box you'll see sample brush strokes that will let you know how the brushes listed in the Artist's Materials box will perform using your stylus and paint. To make it easy to identify which application you'll be using for a project, each Artist's Materials box is color-coded—a lavender-purple for Photoshop and a teal-green for Painter.

Throughout the book you'll find helpful Learn More About boxes that will help you find more information about the topics being discussed. When you encounter an orange asterisk after a term or at the end of a sentence, check the Learn More About box on the spread for an entry related to the term or concept discussed in the text.

Sprinkled throughout the book, you'll find four kinds of sidebars. The sidebars identified by an artist palette (as described earlier), a hand with a stylus, an eye, and a paint can. The artist palette (shown earlier) identifies a conceptual tip from the artist-author, the hand with a stylus denotes a sidebar about the tablet and pen, the eye identifies a sidebar about Photoshop and the paint can shows a Painter-related sidebar. In a few places, I've used the stylus icon and the eye or the paint can icon to identify a combined tip that has information about the tablet and Photoshop or Painter. In a few cases I've combined a tip that has information about Photoshop and Painter using the eye and the paint can icons.

Where possible, I've separated technical information into mini-technique

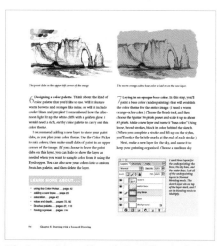

The Artist's Materials boxes are color-coded for Painter and Photoshop.

The Learn More About boxes tell you where you will find more information about a topic.

The Artist's tips are identified by artist palette icons.

sidebars identified by a technique head, such as "Embossing Texture on an Image" on page 146 in Chapter 11. These sidebars are also identified by the warm gold background used on the small sidebars. In several places you'll find tips within a gold-colored sidebar spread that are set off with a white background like the PC/Mac tip below.

Zooming and panning. Use the Zoom Tool (or Magnifier) to zoom in to see areas of detail. When the Brush tool is chosen, you can temporarily switch to the Zoom Tool (or Magnifier) by pressing Ctrl/Cmd-Spacebar. To zoom out, press Ctrl/Cmd-Alt/Option-Spacebar. To pan around a magnified image while painting, you can press the Spacebar to temporarily switch to the Grabber Hand.

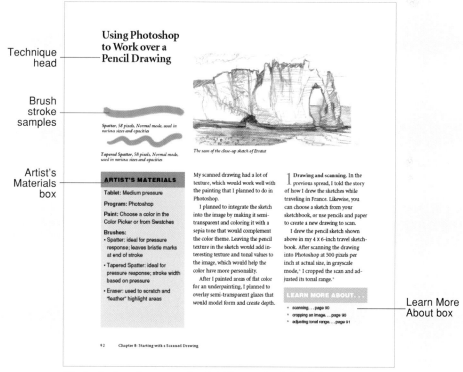

Technique head

Brush stroke samples

Artist's Materials box

Learn More About box

The beginning of an art project is laid out using helpful elements, as you can see here in this page from Chapter 8.

At work in the studio

1

THE DIGITAL ART STUDIO

Here you'll find suggestions for hardware and software and for setting up your studio, whether it's your own studio or in plein air (on location). This chapter also covers making the transition from traditional color theory to digital color tools. Finally, it offers information about pixels, resolution, and desktop fine art printmaking in the studio.

 Your studio is where you come to be creative, so you want it to reflect your personality, with surrounding objects and art that inspire you. My studio has an area with computer equipment for digital work and an area with an easel where I can use conventional art materials. Art decorates the walls, and there are sea shells and photos from my travels, in addition to colorful pottery.

The hardware and software tools have matured to a point that artists are able to use them more intuitively and naturally. Tablets have become more sensitive and easy to use. To make the sensation of drawing on the computer more natural, the stylus has nibs that give you more sensation. For instance, one nib gives the feeling of pencil on paper, and the other nib is spring-loaded, giving the feeling of pushing on a traditional brush with stiff bristles. The programs Painter and Photoshop have become more intuitive to use, and they can sense more nuances of your hand as you draw.

With the digital tools available today, you can become immersed in the painting process more completely, into the line, form, and color of your composition, rather than focusing on the technology when painting on the computer. Think of your digital tools as a new kind of pencil, a new pastel, a new watercolor and a new kind of oil paint.

Setting Up the Digital Art Studio

Working directly on the Cintiq interactive display

First of all, a digital artist's studio is not complete without Painter, Photoshop, and a great-quality tablet.

The software and tablets perform well on both Macintosh and Windows platforms. My first computer was a Mac, and I have always enjoyed the easy-to-use operating system. Today I use G4 and G5 computers for painting and illustration and an iMac for administration. The processor speed is important, as are the amount of RAM and the speed of the hard disk.

Both Photoshop and Painter are "RAM-hungry" applications, so plan to buy lots of RAM for your computer. (My systems have at least 1GB of RAM.) If you're working on a large image and the program uses all of the RAM, the data will spill over to your hard disk. So plan for a fast hard disk to keep performance at its best.

The display you choose is extremely important, both for the care of your eyes and for the quality of your images. Buy the highest-quality display that you can afford. (You'll need a minimum of 17 inches and a video card that will support millions of colors.) My studio has a 23-inch flat panel Apple High-Definition Cinema display and a La Cie 22 Electron Blue with a hood. The hood is helpful for doing color correction and retouching.

If you want to use scans in your art, you'll want to invest in a high-quality scanner. My choice is the Epson Perfection 4870. It features 4800 x 9600 ppi resolution and 48-bit color depth, and it can be used to scan reflective art or transparencies.*

If you want to shoot digital photos to use for reference, I recommend a digital SLR, such as the Canon Digital Rebel, Canon EOS 20D, or Nikon D100.

It's a good idea to invest in a large external hard drive that you can use to safely back up your files. A CD burner is also useful for transferring files and for keeping archives of your work.

Finally, my studio has two inkjet printers: an Epson C86 (for office work and small proofs) and an Epson 2200 for proofs and 13-inch-wide art prints.*

In the studio with the Intuos and Cinema display

Sketching on location using a Toshiba TabletPC and Painter

Shading the screen with an umbrella while painting with an Intuos tablet and Powerbook

PHOTOGRAPHS: MELINDA HOLDEN

To create the paintings described in the book projects, I used Wacom Intuos tablets and a Cintiq.* The Cintiq is a pressure-sensitive LCD that allows you to work directly onscreen. The Cintiq senses 512 pressure levels.

It's also wise to invest in a large, stable desk and a comfortable chair that has arm rests and good lower-back support. (My studio has two 40 x 60-inch desks to hold the computers, monitors, and printers.)

LEARN MORE ABOUT. . .

* working with a scanner. . . page 90
* inkjet printers. . . page 7
* Intuos tablet. . . page 4 and page 13

 Setting up for painting on location. If you want to enjoy sketching outside with a laptop, these tips are for you. The light from the monitor won't compete with natural sunlight. Plan to find a shady spot to set up, or bring a small umbrella that you can use to shield the display. (A hood is also available for some displays.) I set up on a blanket, but you might want to use a folding chair. Two of my favorite times to paint are in the early morning or late afternoon because the shadows are the longest, which contributes to an interesting composition. The photos above show sketching on an early morning that had a soft cloud cover. The gray morning light did not produce long shadows, but it did offer other opportunities, such as the soft gradations in the sky and water and the interesting amber- and ochre-colored forms of the cliffs.

 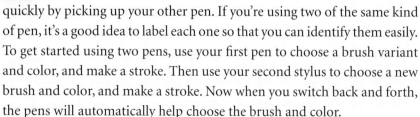 **Using multiple pens.** For more spontaneity while painting, try using two pens when painting in Painter. You can set your Airbrush stylus to be a Digital Airbrush dipped in a color—for instance, blue—and set your grip pen to be the Square Soft Pastel dipped in a second color— green. You can now switch brushes and color quickly by picking up your other pen. If you're using two of the same kind of pen, it's a good idea to label each one so that you can identify them easily. To get started using two pens, use your first pen to choose a brush variant and color, and make a stroke. Then use your second stylus to choose a new brush and color, and make a stroke. Now when you switch back and forth, the pens will automatically help choose the brush and color.

The quick location sketch created in Painter using the TabletPC

The quick location sketch created in Painter using the Intuos

A portable painting studio. You can enjoy the freedom of using a portable digital painting studio for working on location. My favorite tools are a G4 Powerbook and an Intuos tablet. The Intuos tablet supports 1024 levels of pressure, plus tilt, angle, and direction, making the sketching experience very natural.

I have also found a TabletPC to be useful for location work because both the tablet and computer are combined into one compact unit that is easy to carry. The Toshiba TabletPC that I work with uses Wacom's Penabled technology. (Other manufacturers such as Gateway and Panasonic also use Wacom technology.) The TabletPC allows you to work directly onscreen with 512 levels of pressure but doesn't support tilt sensitivity. Still, with just the pressure response, you can create fresh, bold drawings using the Tablet PC unit.

I painted the two images above with the Pastel brushes in Painter. Because the light changes quickly when painting on location, I worked fast, laying in broad areas of color with a Square Soft Pastel, and then adding details with a Tapered Pastel. For more texture, I scumbled using the Square Hard Pastel.* (All of these techniques are described throughout this book.) Although I painted both images using the

Sketching on location using the Intuos tablet and G4 Powerbook

same process and brushes, you'll notice a difference in the texture in the two images. For instance, the image on the left that was painted with the TabletPC has a bolder look, with less subtle texture. The painting on the right shows the delicate paper grain, and the brushstrokes have more variation from thick to thin.

Optional nibs. Two optional stroke nibs are available for the Wacom Grip Pen: a spring-loaded nib that adds tension that feels like a stiff brush, and a felt nib for additional friction between the pen and tablet, much like conventional pencil on paper.

The Power
of Color

For Mendocino Point, *I used dabs of complementary colors in the shadows.*

"Light, that first phenomenon of the world, reveals to us the spirit and living soul of the world through colors." Painter and color theorist Johannes Itten's observation inspires us to think about how color affects not only the appearance of what we see, but also our emotional response to the subject.

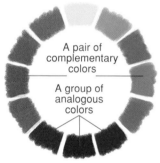

A pair of complementary colors

A group of analogous colors

A pigment-based color wheel with 12 colors

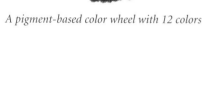

LEARN MORE ABOUT. . .

* scumbling. . . pages 104, 107

Today's color tools are so good that you can make an intuitive transition between traditional color theory and the digital color tools, while enhancing your own personal expression. In this section, we'll take familiar traditional terms and have fun applying them using the digital color tools in Painter and Photoshop.

Hue. The hue is the predominant spectral color, such as yellow or blue-green. Hue indicates a color's position on the color wheel or spectrum and tells us the color's temperature.

Saturation. Also known as intensity or chroma, saturation indicates a color's purity or strength.

Value. A color's lightness or darkness is its luminance or value.

Tint. You can create a tint of a color (lightening it, or increasing its value) by mixing it with white or a lighter color, or in the case of transparent washes, you can dilute the color with a clear medium like water.

Shade. You can mix a shade of a color (darkening it, or decreasing its value) by adding a darker color. To use a tonalist approach, you might want to add dark gray or black. I carefully observe the shadows when I'm painting, and often build the shadows by adding dabs of a darker complementary color to them. See "Color Inspiration and Interpretation" on page 163 for more information.

A blue color at full saturation (top), and a tint and a shade of the color

A blue color at full saturation (top), and a tint and a shade of the color

Tints, shades, and saturation in Painter. To choose a hue in Painter from the Colors palette, click in the Hue Ring. To create a tint of the color, move the little circle higher in the Saturation/Value triangle in the Colors palette. To create a shade of a color, move the little circle lower in the Saturation/Value triangle.

To adjust the saturation of the color, move to the right in the Saturation/Value triangle to increase saturation or move to the left to decrease it.

Tints, shades, and saturation in Photoshop. You can choose a hue from the Color palette or the Color Picker. I've used the Color Picker here because it's more intuitive to select a hue and then make a tint or shade of the color. Click on the Foreground Color in the Toolbox to open the Color Picker, and choose a hue in the vertical Color slider. To choose a tint, click higher in the large Color field, and click lower to choose a shade.

To adjust the saturation of a color in Photoshop, move to the right in the Color field to increase the saturation or move to the left to decrease it.

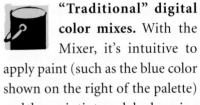 **"Traditional" digital color mixes.** With the Mixer, it's intuitive to apply paint (such as the blue color shown on the right of the palette) and then mix tints and shades using colors from the color wells or the Colors palette.

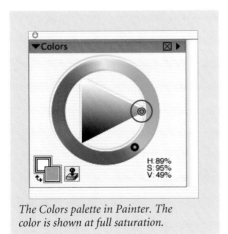

The Colors palette in Painter. The color is shown at full saturation.

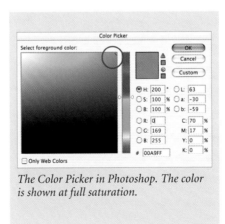

The Color Picker in Photoshop. The color is shown at full saturation.

Using the Mix Color tool in Painter's Mixer palette to create tints and shades

Pixels and Image Resolution

Peppers *study, painted using Painter*

Images created in Photoshop and Painter are pixel based. Pixels are square elements arranged in a grid that builds the image file. The resolution of an image is determined by the number of pixels per inch (ppi).

Resolution is a term that describes the number of pixels, or the amount of data in a bitmap (raster) image file. Illustrations created in programs like Adobe Illustrator or Corel Draw are vector based. Vector-based images consist of mathematical instructions that describe vectors, rather than pixels. Vector graphics are scalable and transformable, without loss of quality. Pixel-based images, on the other hand, are resolution dependent, which means that quality can suffer if the image resolution is too low for the size and method of printing that is used.

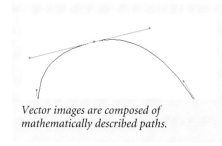

Vector images are composed of mathematically described paths.

How will the image be used? Before beginning an illustration, it's a good idea to plan ahead: How will you present your image? Will it appear in a book or magazine that is printed using an offset press? Will it be printed on an inkjet printer at a fine art service bureau? Will you print your image on your own studio inkjet? Take this planning into account when you are starting a new file, or when you are scanning images (or shooting digital photos) that you will use to create a composite illustration.

Resolution for offset printing. This book was printed using a four-color commercial offset printing process. I created the images at their final dimensions at a resolution of 300 pixels per inch. To be printed on an offset press, the square pixels are converted into a grid of round dots for half tones. The (half tone) line screen used for this book is 150 lpi (lines per inch).

To figure out how large a file you should start with, you need to know the line screen. Typical line-screen resolutions are 56 lpi (screen printing), 85 lpi (newspaper), 133 lpi, 150 lpi, and 200 lpi (magazines and

The New dialog box in Photoshop showing the dimensions and the resolution

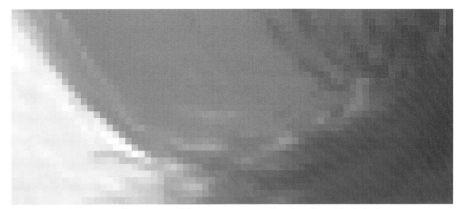

Peppers study; detail shown at 300%

A 1600% enlargement of a portion of the peppers image showing the grid of pixels

books). If your line screen is 150 lpi, it's recommended that you multiply the line-screen number (150) by two. Two is a conservative factor to use, and this would create an image resolution of 300 ppi.

Resolution for inkjet printing.

When creating an image file to print on my Epson 2000P, I set up the file at its final dimensions (for instance, 20 x 16 inches), with a resolution between 150–300 pixels per inch. I've not noticed improvement in quality with settings higher than 200 pixels per inch.

Prior to creating an image file that will be printed at a fine art service bureau, speak with your service bureau to find out the equipment requirements. Service bureaus use equipment from different manufacturers—for instance, Iris, Epson, Hewlett-Packard, and Roland. The printing equipment might require different resolutions, and some might require that you convert your RGB file to CMYK color mode (like the Iris, for instance).*

 Resizing, resampling, and interpolation. The illustrations below show the Image Size dialog box in Photoshop (Image > Image Size). Painter has a similar dialog box (Canvas > Resize). The dialog box on the left is set up to resize an image. Resizing changes the physical dimensions of a file, without changing the number of pixels in the file. Resampling, however, uses a process called interpolation to increase or decrease the number of pixels in the file. Resampling can cause softness and artifacts in a file. It's recommended not to resample "up" more than 10%. Resampling down is less harmful to the file, but some sharpening might be needed. When you're using interpolation, Photoshop and Painter remap pixels to enlarge or reduce the size of the image. If you enlarge the image, new pixels are manufactured. Pixels are discarded when you resample to a smaller size.

* inkjet printing. . . page 9
* color modes. . . page 42

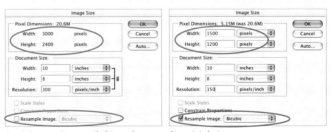

Resizing an image (left) and resampling (right)

Fine Art Printmaking in the Studio

I made an artist proof of Along Tomales Bay *on an Epson 2200*

Many affordable alternatives are available for artists who want to proof their images or make fine art prints in their own studio using archival inks and papers.

Today's desktop inkjet printers deliver beautiful color prints. The affordable HP printers (such as the DesignJet 30 and 130) and the Epson printers (the C86 and the 2200, for instance) are good printers not only for pulling test prints before sending images to a fine art service bureau, but also for use in experimental fine art printmaking.

The Epson 2200 ships with a seven-color UltraChrome pigmented inkset, and it produces water-resistant prints, especially when used with Epson's Enhanced Matte or Somerset Velvet for Epson paper. If you'd like to experiment on them by applying pastel or acrylic paint, these prints will accept the media without smearing or running.

Many traditional art papers are now manufactured for digital printmaking—for instance, Arches, Crane Museo, Somerset, Concorde Rag, and Hahnemuehle's German Etching papers, which are available from Cone Editions' Ink Jet Mall or Digital Art Supplies. Also, new canvases are available for use with inkjet printers. For instance, check out the artist-grade

 Larger format prints. If you're looking for a larger format printer, the Epson 4000 is an excellent choice. It is a desktop seven-color inkjet printer that uses the Epson UltraChrome pigmented inks. It handles media from 17 inches wide with an unlimited length. It can handle heavier substrates, up to cardboard 1.5 mm thick. Another alternative, the Hewlett-Packard DesignJet 130 is a six-color dye-based printer that can print on papers up to 24 x 64 inches.

canvases available from Digital Art Supplies, located on the web at www.digitalartsupplies.com.

Henry Wilhelm has done important research regarding the longevity of different ink and substrate combinations. A comparison of longevity with the different inks and papers is available through Wilhelm Imaging Research, Inc., on the web at www.wilhelm-research.com.

You can find more information on these topics in the "Printmaking and Archival Concerns" chapter of *The Painter Wow! Book.*

 Fine art print studios. You can order large exhibition-quality prints from a digital printmaking studio such as Cone Editions Press, High Resolution, and Trillium Press. In the Appendix in the back of this book, you'll find a selective list of printmakers that trusted colleagues and I have worked with.

Favorite art materials

2

PHOTOSHOP, PAINTER, AND TABLET BASICS FOR ARTISTS

Here you'll find instructions for setting up your tablet, drawing and navigating with the tablet and stylus, customizing your workspace, and more. Both Painter and Photoshop have brushes, color tools, layers, blend modes, and methods for isolating portions of images, but each program has its own strengths. In the individual sections that are devoted to Photoshop and Painter, you'll find definitions of terms and some comparisons between the two programs.

 The Wacom Intuos tablet and stylus provides the freedom to paint with a cordless pen and communicate the expressive nuances of hand and wrist movements to the computer through programs like Painter and Photoshop. Without a fine-quality tablet and stylus, I could not create the paintings that you see in this book. I choose to use the Intuos line of tablets because they allow sensitivity that other tablets do not, such as higher levels of pressure sensitivity, tilt, bearing, and other movements. Without this complex sensitivity, the brushes in Painter and Photoshop would not perform the way you see them pictured in the illustrations that demonstrate the brushstrokes. I'm amazed at how good Photoshop is with compositing, color correction, and painting. Painter continues to delight me with its incredible variety of realistic natural media, textures, and special effects that I enjoy using with my paintings. Together with the tablet, these two programs make up the perfect work environment for a fine artist or an illustrator.

Introduction

This chapter is not meant to cover everything basic about the tools used in this book—it focuses on favorite features of the hardware and software that are useful for artists who want to paint.

Photoshop and Painter overlap in some areas of functionality, and they both have unique strengths. Both programs have brushes and features for working with color, layers, and selections. *Layers* are elements that hover above the image background, providing a great deal of flexibility in composing artwork. A *selection* is an area of the image that has been isolated so that changes can be made to the contents only, or to protect the area from change. You'll find more information on these topics later in this chapter and in the projects that follow.

Portability. The portability between Photoshop and Painter has improved. You can now move files with layers, layer masks, and alpha channels between the programs with the layers intact—if you remember a few basic rules. To take a Photoshop file into Painter, save your working Photoshop file in Photoshop format to preserve the native effects and functions such as layer styles and adjustment layers. Then make a copy of your working file with the layers converted to pixel-based layers, and save it in Photoshop format for opening in Painter. When working in Painter, always save your working Painter file in RIFF format (Painter's native format). RIFF format preserves Painter's native brush effects such as "wet" Watercolor paint, thick Impasto paint, special effects layers, and other native effects. If you'd like to take a Painter file into Photoshop, save a copy of the file in Photoshop format with any special layers (such as adjustment layers or layer styles) converted to default (pixel-based) layers. Chapter 14 demonstrates working between Photoshop and Painter.

Strengths of Photoshop. My favorite Photoshop features are its efficient selection tools, masking and layer organization, retouching and color tools, and brushes. If you need to retouch, or if you enjoy collaging elements in your art, you need Photoshop.

Strengths of Painter. Painter was created for artists who draw and paint. The natural media brushes, textures, and color palettes are central to Painter, as are its unique special effects. Also, Painter's brushes can sense more of the subtle movements of your hand while drawing with a tablet. If you're serious about painting on the computer, you need Painter.

Anatomy of a Tablet and Stylus

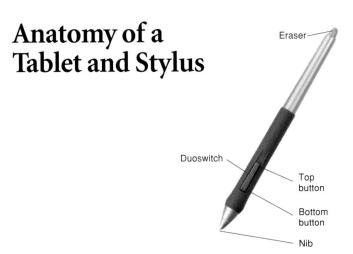

The Intuos3 grip pen

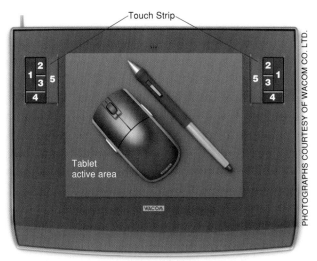

The 6 x 8 Intuos3 tablet shown with the mouse and pen

The Intuos tablet. Without a quality tablet, I could not have created the beautiful paintings in Painter and Photoshop that you'll see in the projects and gallery later in this book. You will not achieve the full performance of the brushes with just the software and a mouse. The Intuos tablets feature 1024 levels of pressure, and they sense subtle variations in your wrist and arm movements—such as tilt and bearing—that other tablets do not. The Intuos3 offers a resolution of 5080 lines per inch, which allows for greater accuracy while navigating and drawing.

The illustrations above show important features of the Intuos3 tablet. If you have an earlier Intuos tablet, the shaft buttons on the stylus operate the same as the Intuos3. The Duoswitch is a shaft button that rocks, depending on the area that you activate. On earlier tablets, the tablet buttons are across the top. Although they provide helpful functions, the Intuos3 tablet provides much more.

The Graphire tablet. If you have a small budget, the Graphire tablet might be a good choice; however, it's not as sensitive as the Intuos line. The Graphire features 512 levels of pressure (compared to the Intuos 1024) and it is not capable of sensing other movements.

A less-cluttered desktop with the Intuos3. If you learn to use the ExpressKeys* while painting, you can eliminate the use of your keyboard during most painting tasks. The illustration above shows the ExpressKeys and Touch Strips with numbers. You can modify the tablet preferences to customize the keys. The default settings are as follows. The numbers correspond to those in the figure above:

1. Control modifier for Windows and Command (Apple key) for Mac lets you switch from the Brush tool to the Move tool (Photoshop) or Layer Adjuster (Painter).

2. Shift modifier key.

3. Alt/Option lets you switch from the Brush tool to the Eyedropper and sample color in Photoshop or Painter.

4. Space key (spacebar) lets you pan around the image.

5. Touch Strip: By default, the Touch Strips zoom in and out of the image in Painter and Photoshop. Slide your hand up to zoom in and slide down to zoom out. To zoom in one field, tap near the top end of the Touch Strip. To zoom out one field, tap near the bottom end of the Touch Strip.

*ExpressKeys™ is a registered trademark of Ginsan Industries and is used by Wacom with permission.

Getting Started with Your Tablet

Sitting up straight while painting, with the arms of the chair adjusted to match the table

GETTING COMFORTABLE WITH YOUR TABLET

The photograph above shows me using my tablet at my desk. I recommend choosing a chair that has an adjustable back and arms because working on the computer requires a lot of sitting. (When working on the computer, remember to get up and take breaks to stretch.) Notice how I have the arms of the chair adjusted to match the height of the pull-out shelf on my desk. I adjusted the chair height so that I could align the arms of the chair with the pull-out on the desk. This setup keeps my arms supported and relaxed while working. If I'm making wide, expressive strokes on a larger tablet, such as a 12 X 12, I lower the chair arms so that I can sweep broadly with my hand. If I'm doing a lot of typing, I place my keyboard on the tablet. When I'm painting, the keyboard is on the table above the tablet, as shown in the photo.

It helps to sit up straight when you're painting. You'll have more energy. It's so easy to get lost in your art and slump in the chair. Other times, I place my tablet in my lap when I want to relax and draw. I find that this position feels similar to sketching with my conventional sketchbook on my lap.

In addition to helping you draw more expressively on the computer, you can use your stylus as a useful, comfortable pointing device when you need to choose a command from a menu or to move a palette around on the screen. It feels more natural in your hand than a mouse. Spreading your hand and pushing a mouse for hours can lead to wrist problems. I prefer to use my stylus for drawing and some of the pointing tasks because it keeps my hand from getting overworked.

Photo of the artist's hand in a comfortable position for drawing

DRAWING AND NAVIGATING WITH THE STYLUS

Follow the manufacturer's directions for connecting the tablet to your computer and for installing the tablet software. The top left of the tablet is orientated to the top left of your display.

Navigating using Pen mode. By default, your tablet will be set up in Pen mode, which is the mode you'll want to use for drawing. With Pen mode, the cursor will jump to wherever you move it on the screen using absolute positioning, which means that every point on your tablet corresponds to exactly one point on the screen. If you'd like to choose a color, lift the stylus up from the tablet and point to a new color in the Colors palette (touch once on it). Lift up the pen and touch it back onto your image where you want to paint. Then press and draw across the tablet to make a brushstroke. To move a palette onscreen, first point to the item to select it and then drag it to move it.

Making brushstrokes. To draw in Photoshop, choose the Brush tool in the Toolbox. A brush will automatically be chosen, but if you'd like to use another brush, open the Brush Preset Picker on the Options Bar and select a brush preset. To draw in Painter, choose the Brush tool in the Toolbox. A brush will automatically be available, but if you'd like to use another one, choose a brush category (such as the Pencils) from the Brush Selector Bar, and then choose a variant (such as the 2B Pencil variant of Pencils).

Hold your stylus in your hand comfortably, similar to how you would hold a pencil or conventional pen. (You can hover the pen over the tablet to reposition the cursor if needed.) Touch your stylus to your tablet and press down, keeping your pen in contact with the tablet as you complete the first brushstroke. Lift up to start another brushstroke.

To achieve the brushstrokes you'd like to paint, you might have to press harder with your stylus on the tablet than you're accustomed to pressing down on a pencil when you're drawing on paper.

 Keeping a safe distance. If you want to take a break from drawing, or if you need to use your mouse, move your stylus off the tablet surface so that the tablet will not sense it. (The stylus will become active when it is approximately 6mm or .25 inches from the tablet surface.)

Using a Tapered Pastel brush in Painter, I drew these brushstrokes. I used a default Medium Tip Feel setting for the top stroke and my favorite medium-soft setting for the bottom stroke.

CHOOSING YOUR SETTINGS FOR YOUR STYLUS

Taking a look at important settings. After you have connected your tablet to your computer and have installed the software, you can open the tablet application and begin learning about the settings. The driver dialog box has been redesigned for the new Intuos3 tablet. If you have an earlier tablet, the settings are similar (for instance, the Intuos2). If you have already begun to use your tablet and want to follow this exercise, I recommend resetting the tablet application to its global defaults by clicking the Reset Tab to Default button.

Adjusting the Tip Feel tab. In my opinion, the Tip Feel tab is the most important window because its settings affect how Photoshop and Painter interpret the pressure that you apply to the tablet. The Tip Feel controls the hardness or softness of the pressure curve. The harder the pressure curve, the firmer you'll have to press on the tablet to make a brushstroke appear on your screen, and the less variation in the stroke. With a softer curve, you'll

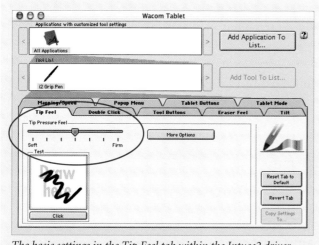

The basic settings in the Tip Feel tab within the Intuos2 driver window

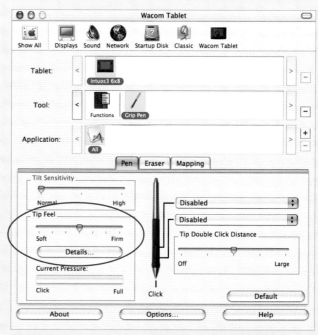

The Tip Feel controls under the Pen tab in the Intuos3 driver window

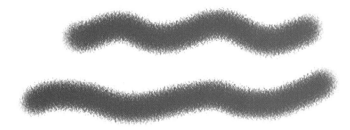

I drew the top Tapered Pastel brushstroke using the firmest Tip Feel setting, and it required that I press very firmly to make a mark. I drew the bottom stroke using the softest setting using very light pressure.

be able to draw by applying much less pressure. As you can see by looking at the illustration above, if you choose a setting that is too hard or too soft, you'll lose the delicate, expressive control you need. When you experiment with the range of Tip Feel settings in the Wacom Tablet window, you might find out that you prefer different settings for Photoshop and Painter, as I do. In the projects that follow later in this book, you'll notice suggested tablet settings listed in the Artist's Materials boxes. To learn about customizing the buttons on the stylus for expressive sketching, turn to the next page.

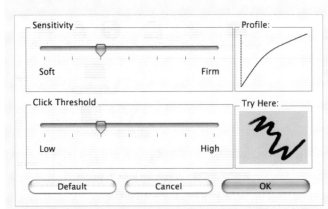

The Details window (for the Intuos3) displays a Sensitivity Profile for the stroke, and it allows you to draw a test stroke.

Customizing settings for applications. You can set up specific preferences for your favorite application. First, launch the programs for which you want to arrange settings. In the Wacom Tablet window, click on the tool you want to customize (I chose the Grip Pen icon) and then click the small plus to the right of the Applications field. The Select Application window will appear. Make a choice from the list of applications, and click OK. Back in the Wacom Tablet window, click on the application you want to arrange, and then adjust the settings. (I clicked on the Adobe Photoshop CS icon and on the Pen tab and adjusted the

Tip Feel for a harder pressure curve. Then, because I like a softer pressure curve with Painter's brushes, I clicked on the Corel Painter IX icon and adjusted the Tip Feel settings for this program.)

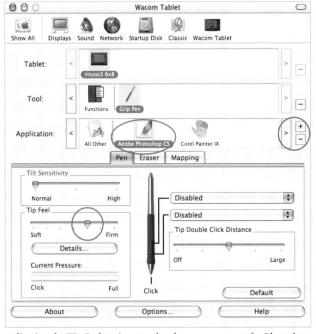

Adjusting the Tip Feel settings to a harder pressure curve for Photoshop

Quick sketch drawn in Painter with the Cover Pencil

Coloring the sketch with loose brushstrokes of pastel and chalk

Customizing the buttons on the stylus for expressive sketching. Next, configure the tool buttons on the pen (for all applications). Click the Tool Buttons tab (the Pen tab for the Intuos3). For the top button on the stylus, leave the button set to Erase. While doing expressive sketching, I often roll the stylus in my hand, which makes it easy to accidentally push one of the buttons while holding the stylus. For the exercises and projects in

Chapters 3–7, I recommend setting the two shaft buttons to Disabled (or Ignored) because an artist holds this area of the pen while drawing. For more methodical work such as painting subtle, graduated values, you can set the shaft buttons to help you to sample color while you're painting.

The tablet is automatically mapped to fit the screen on the computer where it is installed, as shown below.

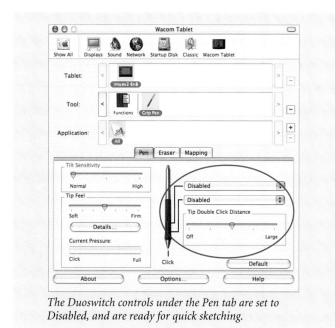

The Duoswitch controls under the Pen tab are set to Disabled, and are ready for quick sketching.

The Mapping tab showing the Mode set to Pen, Screen and Tablet areas set to Full

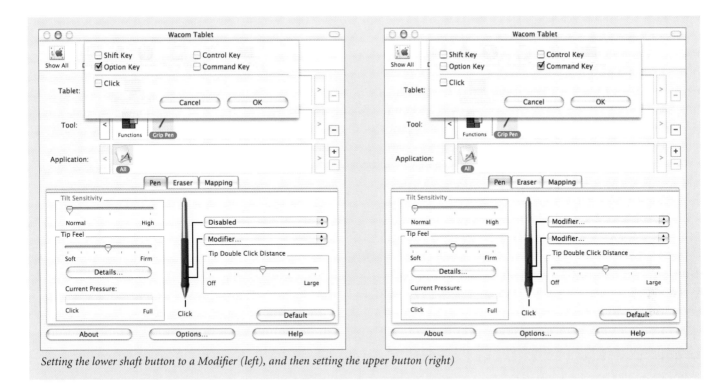

Setting the lower shaft button to a Modifier (left), and then setting the upper button (right)

CUSTOMIZING THE STYLUS BUTTONS

Setting the Duoswitch pen shaft buttons to sample color. When doing quick sketching, I prefer to set my stylus buttons to Disabled (or Ignored) so that I don't accidentally press them if I am rolling the pen in my hand. For doing more sustained work, it's helpful to set up the buttons so that you can sample color on-the-fly in Photoshop and Painter by toggling from the Brush tool to the Eyedropper tool. In the Wacom window, click on the Pen tab; then click the pop-up menu for the upper shaft button, and choose Alt (PC) or Option (Mac). Click OK.

Setting a pen shaft button to help adjust a layer. You can set up the second shaft button to temporarily switch from the Brush tool to the Move tool in Photoshop or to the Layer Adjuster in Painter. In the Pen tab, click on the lower shaft button pop-up menu, and choose Control (PC users) or Command (Mac). If you do more compositing work with layers in Photoshop and more of your painting in Painter, it's a good idea to set up your tablet preferences to reflect how you use the pen in each program. You might want to program your pen Duoswitch to use the modifiers for Photoshop (to quickly reposition a layer on your image) and then set the Duoswitch to be disabled in Painter while you're painting.

 A helpful eraser. It's a good idea to leave the button on the top end of the stylus set to function as an Eraser (its default setting) so that you can turn your pen upside down and erase on-the-fly.

 Making a Wacom shortcut. To quickly access your tablet settings, consider making a shortcut or an alias for the Wacom application.

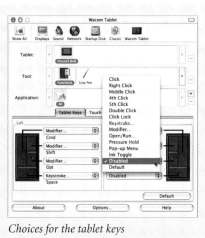

Choices for the tablet keys

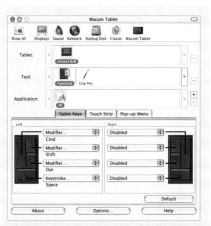

Pressing a tablet key to sample color while painting

CUSTOMIZING BUTTONS ON AN INTUOS3 TABLET

Setting up for your non-dominant hand. By default, the Intuos3 tablet is set up with the ExpressKeys and Touch Strips on both sides of the tablet enabled. You can program the tablet buttons so that you are using only the buttons on the side for your nondominant hand. For instance, I paint with my right hand; therefore, I usually set the buttons on the right side of the tablet to Disabled so that I don't accidentally activate one of

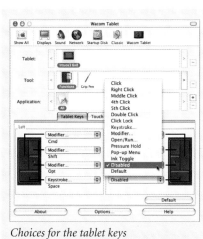

The keys on the right are disabled for an artist who draws with the pen in the right hand.

them if I rest my hand on that side of the tablet while drawing. While I'm drawing, I can use my non dominant hand on the buttons on the left side of the tablet. For instance, the number 3 key (with the dot) by default is set to Alt/Option. While painting with a brush in Painter or Photoshop, I can press the number 3 key to toggle from the brush to the Eyedropper to sample color from my image as I work. In addition, you can set the Touch Strips to accept input from the pen only.

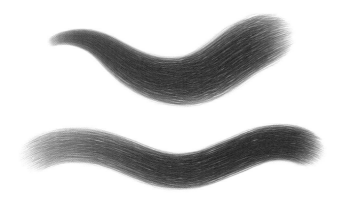

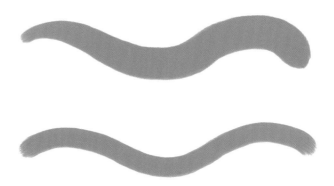

Brushstrokes painted in Painter using the Thick Acrylic Round. Top: varied pressure; bottom: pressure controlled by the Pressure Hold key.

Strokes painted in Photoshop using the Gouache brush from Chapter 9. Top: varied pressure; bottom: pressure controlled using the Pressure Hold key.

Setting a tablet key to control pressure. You can set your tablet so that you can retain a particular amount of pressure on-the-fly while you are drawing a brushstroke. Click on Functions in the Wacom window and choose the Tablet Keys tab. Choose a key you want to program, click its pop-up menu, and choose Pressure Hold. After setting up your Pressure Hold key, try making some brushstrokes in each program. Begin making a stroke,

and then press the key to retain the pressure you were applying at that moment. To draw a thinner stroke on-the-fly without changing your brush size, press the key and then begin painting the stroke.

 Changing the size of a brush using tablet keys. You can set the tablet keys on an Intuos3 to the bracket keys, which are a shortcut in Photoshop for changing brush size. (Press the left bracket key [to reduce the size. To increase its size, use the right bracket].) In the Wacom window, click on Functions. When the window appears, choose a key and select Keystroke from its pop-up menu. When the Keystroke menu appears, choose [and click OK. To set a key to increase the brush size, use] and follow the same process as before.

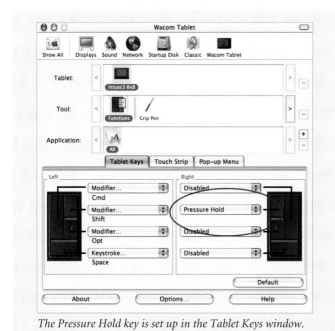

The Pressure Hold key is set up in the Tablet Keys window.

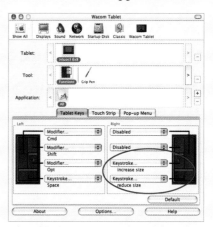

The tablet keys are set to the keystrokes.

Using the stylus wheel on the airbrush pen to control the flow of media while painting

Airbrush Hard Round strokes (from left to right), button near to forward, midway, and all the way back

USING THE AIRBRUSH STYLUS

A special Wacom stylus. The Wacom Intuos Airbrush* stylus has a fingerwheel that provides additional control over the application of paint. You can operate the wheel independently of the pressure, tilt, or angle you apply to the stylus. Hold the stylus comfortably in your hand, and touch it to your tablet. Use your index finger to roll the wheel forward to reduce the flow of paint and backward to increase the flow of paint. In addition, both Photoshop and Painter have settings that take advantage of the fingerwheel. Many of the presets in Photoshop and the brush variants in Painter can be set to take advantage of the Airbrush stylus controls.

Adjusting size with the stylus wheel in Photoshop. You can set the Airbrush Hard Round so that the stylus wheel controls the width of the stroke. In the Brushes palette's Shape Dynamics window, set the Size Jitter Control pop-up menu to Stylus Wheel.

The Airbrush Hard Round and the Shape Dynamics pane of the Brushes palette

Another dimension. If you have a tool and brushes that support rotation, you can enjoy more variety with your brushstrokes. Pay a visit to the book's web site at www.peachpit.com/tabletbook for more information.

LEARN MORE ABOUT. . .

* Airbrushes. . . page 150

Airbrush Soft Round strokes, from left to right: button near to forward, midway, and all the way back

Digital Airbrush strokes, from left to right: button near to forward, midway, and all the way back

Fine Spray Airbrush strokes, from left to right: button near to forward, midway, and all the way back

Adjusting media flow with the stylus wheel in Photoshop. You can set the Airbrush Soft Round (and other presets) so the stylus wheel controls the amount of media applied. Open the Brushes palette, and in the Other Dynamics window, set the Control pop-up menu to Stylus Wheel.

Adjusting size with the stylus wheel in Painter. You can set the Digital Airbrush (and other Airbrushes in Painter) so that the stylus wheel controls the stroke width. In the Size section of the Brush Creator, set the Size Expression pop-up menu to Wheel and the Min Size to about 20%.

Adjusting media flow with the stylus wheel in Painter. You can set the Fine Spray, Coarse Spray, and a few other Airbrushes so that the stylus wheel controls the amount of media applied. In the Airbrush section of the Brush Creator, set the Expression pop-up menu to Wheel.

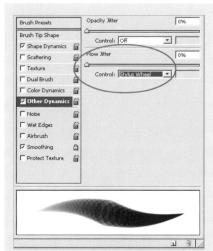

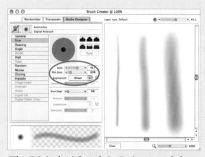

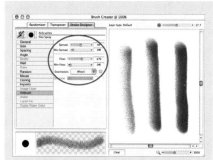

The Airbrush Soft Round and the Other Dynamics pane of the Brushes palette

The Digital Airbrush in Painter and the Size section of the Brush Creator

The Fine Spray Airbrush in Painter and the Airbrush section of the Brush Creator

Photoshop Basics for Painters

Rather than focus on the nuances of every tool in Photoshop, this section focuses on the basics of Photoshop with painters in mind. Here, you'll find information and tips about brushes and tools that take advantage of the tablet. This section includes an overview of the interface, information about the Brushes palette and Color palettes, helpful tips for painters, and ideas for customizing your Photoshop workspace.

Let's begin with an overview of the Photoshop interface. By default, the Toolbox displays 22 tools. When you see an arrow in the lower right of a tool's field, click and hold, and the tools that are nested underneath the top tool will pop out.

The Options Bar is a context-sensitive palette at the top of the Photoshop screen that shows the settings for the current tool. In the upper right of the Options Bar, you'll notice a docking area where you can store often-used palettes.

 Hide and show. Press the Tab key to hide or show the Toolbox and all of the palettes that are open.

PHOTOSHOP'S TOOLBOX

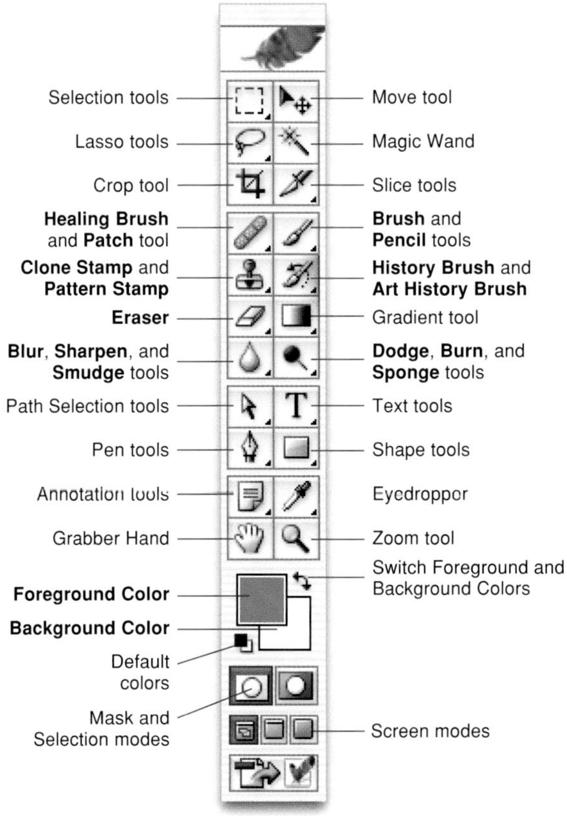

Selection tools		Move tool
Lasso tools		Magic Wand
Crop tool		Slice tools
Healing Brush and **Patch** tool		**Brush** and **Pencil** tools
Clone Stamp and **Pattern Stamp**		**History Brush** and **Art History Brush**
Eraser		Gradient tool
Blur, **Sharpen**, and **Smudge** tools		**Dodge**, **Burn**, and **Sponge** tools
Path Selection tools		Text tools
Pen tools		Shape tools
Annotation tools		Eyedropper
Grabber Hand		Zoom tool
		Switch Foreground and Background Colors
Foreground Color		
Background Color		
Default colors		
Mask and Selection modes		Screen modes

The Toolbox with a focus on the painting, toning, and focus tools that have controls that you can set up for a tablet

The pen offers more control than the mouse when using Photoshop. I painted these two brushstrokes with the Hard Round 19 pixels preset from Photoshop's default brushes. I painted the red brushstroke with a stylus and tablet and the blue brushstroke using a mouse.

THE PHOTOSHOP WORKSPACE

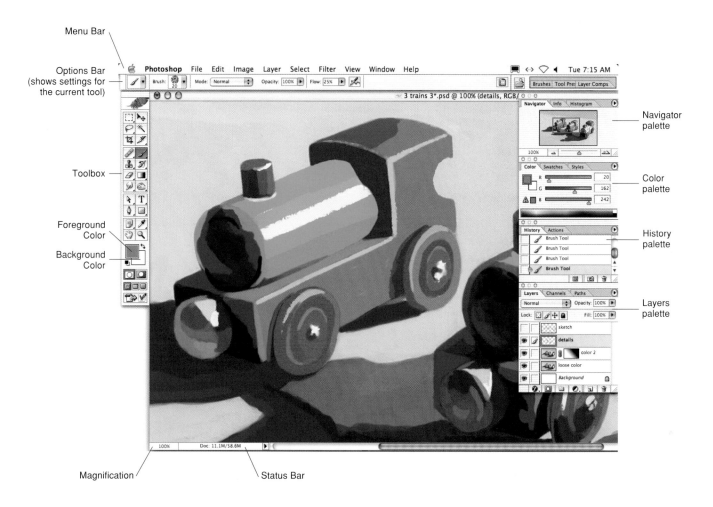

Menu Bar

Options Bar
(shows settings for
the current tool)

Toolbox

Foreground
Color

Background
Color

Navigator
palette

Color
palette

History
palette

Layers
palette

Magnification

Status Bar

Four palette groups are docked on the right when you first launch Photoshop. The Navigator palette is useful for panning around a magnified image. The Colors palette displays sliders that you can adjust to mix color, or you can choose color by clicking in the Color Bar at the bottom of the palette. The History palette allows you to click back in history states and can function as a multiple undo alternative. Next, the Layers palette allows you to store and manage elements that float above your image background.

The magnification of the document is displayed in the lower-left corner of the Photoshop window (100% magnification displays your image with the most accuracy). The Status Bar lets you view the Document size, Scratch sizes, Timing information, and Efficiency information.

For The Three Engines, *I created swatches to store my colors and then painted on layers.*

Helpful palettes. The Layers palette lets you organize the floating elements in your illustrations. For flexibility, you can paint individual elements on their own layers if you like and then hide or show them or move them around. I tend to create an underpainting on its own layer and then add refined values and details on their own layers, as shown in *The Three Engines.* The computer provides flexibility that suits our own workflow.

With the Color palette, you can choose color. Click in the Color Bar to choose a color, or use the sliders. If you have a series of illustrations with the same color theme, the Swatches palette is a useful place to store the colors.

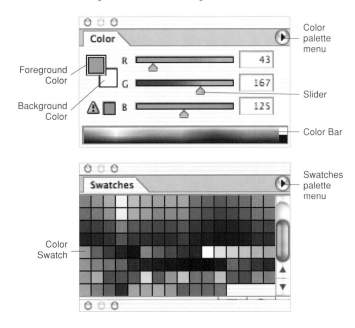

When painting Sunrise, *I used blending modes and reduced opacities for delicate color mixes.*

You can see the transparent glazes in this detail.

The Brushes palette. With the Brushes palette, you can chose a preset brush or create your own custom brush and save it as a new brush preset. You can use the brush presets with the Brush and Pencil tools; the Clone Stamp and Pattern Stamp tools; the Dodge, Burn, and Sponge tools; and the Blur, Sharpen and Smudge tools. On the left of the palette, under Brush Tip Shape, are the names of windows where more important controls are located. You'll learn about them in the section "Customizing Brushes," which follows.

 Trying out blending modes. To quickly cycle through the blending modes in the Options Bar when you want to experiment with different brushstroke looks, press Shift - (hyphen) to move up the list and Shift + to move down it.

 A white image background color. For the projects in this book, it is preferable to set Background Contents to white in the New dialog box when you begin a project.

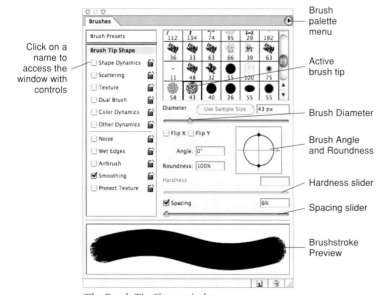

The Brush Tip Shape window

Click on a name to access the window with controls

Brush palette menu

Active brush tip

Brush Diameter

Brush Angle and Roundness

Hardness slider

Spacing slider

Brushstroke Preview

Set the Background Contents to white in the New dialog box.

Brushstroke painted with the default Spatter 59 pixels preset

The shape of the brushstroke changes based on the pressure you apply.

CUSTOMIZING BRUSHES

You can modify a default brush preset to change its stroke width and opacity based on the pressure you apply to the stylus. To try out the brush settings, begin by choosing the Brush tool in the Toolbox and opening the Brushes palette (Window > Brushes).

 **A helpful view.** To set up the Brushes palette with a list view for easier access to the brush presets, choose Small List from the Brush palette menu.

Choosing Small List view

Choosing a brush and painting a stroke. In the Brushes palette, click on Brush Presets and scroll down the list to find the Spatter 59 pixels preset. Use your stylus to paint a squiggly brushstroke. You'll see an opaque stroke with some stray bristle hairs.

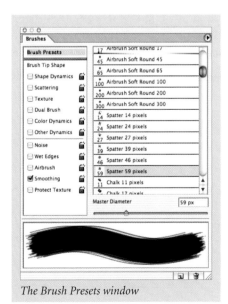

The Brush Presets window

Setting the brush to change its stroke width. Back in the Brushes palette, click on Shape Dynamics. In this window, set the Size Jitter Control pop-up menu to Pen Pressure. Make another squiggly stroke, and you'll see the thickness vary based on the pressure that you apply.

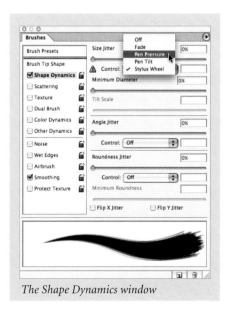

The Shape Dynamics window

The shape and the opacity of the brushstroke change based on the pressure you apply.

Strokes of a second color demonstrate the varied opacity and the mixing of color.

The rain strokes in the sky of the Little Wolf study were painted with a custom Spatter brush.

Setting the brush to change its opacity. In the Brushes palette, click on Other Dynamics and set the Opacity Jitter Control pop-up menu to Pen Pressure. Make another stroke using varied pressure, and you'll see the opacity vary based on the pressure you use. Save the Brush preset.*

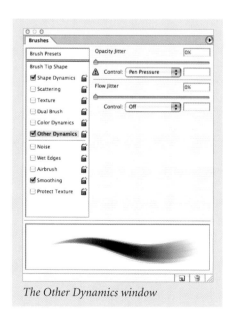

The Other Dynamics window

Trying out the brush with more colors. For this exercise, make sure that the paint Mode menu in the Options Bar is set to Normal. Now that you have a brush that will change opacity and stroke width based on pressure, paint a few more brushstrokes using different colors. You'll be able to create the look of semitransparent washes with delicate color mixes. By varying the pressure on your stylus, you can achieve a broad range from translucent to opaque.

The Mode menu in the Options Bar

LEARN MORE ABOUT. . .

* airbrush pen fingerwheel. . . page 22
* saving a brush preset. . . pages 97, 116
* Tapered Spatter brush. . . page 97
* Airbrush Soft Round. . . page 150

You'll find examples of variations of this brush used in the projects in Chapters 8 and 11. In the *Little Wolf* study, I painted soft clouds using a custom Airbrush Soft Round preset, and then I used the custom Tapered Spatter brush to paint angled strokes of varied opacity for the effect of rain.* You can achieve different transparent paint looks using various blend modes, such as Multiply, Soft Light, Overlay, and Color Burn.

The controls described here are used to create many of the custom brushes that are described in the projects later in this book.

 More control. All of the Control pop-up menus in the Brushes palette can be set to Off, Fade, Pen Pressure, Pen Tilt, or Stylus Wheel. (The Stylus Wheel operates with the airbrush pen fingerwheel.)*

Brushstroke painted using firm pressure

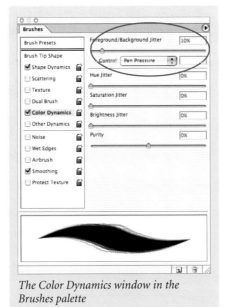

Brushstroke painted using varied lighter pressure

More dynamic color. You can paint with multiple colors by enabling Color Dynamics. Choose a foreground and a background color that are different in the Toolbox. In the Brushes palette, choose the custom Spatter preset that you made on the preceding page. In the Brushes palette, click on Color Dynamics. Set the Control pop-up menu to Pen Pressure; then set the Foreground/Background Color Jitter slider to about 10%. Using firm pressure on your stylus, make a squiggly brushstroke. Make another

brushstroke using varied light-to-heavy pressure. Experiment with the other settings. Hue Jitter, Saturation Jitter, Brightness Jitter, and Purity provide more interesting color opportunities.

 Saving a new brush library. To avoid losing custom brushes when you reset Photoshop to defaults or do a reinstall, it's a good idea to save your custom brushes into your own library. To save a new brush library, choose Save Brushes from the pop-out menu on the Brushes palette. Name your new brush library. To have it appear in the list of brush libraries at the bottom of the Brushes palette in Photoshop CS, save it into the Brushes folder within the Presets folder in the Adobe Photoshop application folder.

Saving your files. When working in Photoshop, save your files in Photoshop format for the best performance and to preserve the program's native layers and effects, such as adjustment layers.

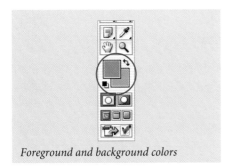

Foreground and background colors

The Color Dynamics window in the Brushes palette

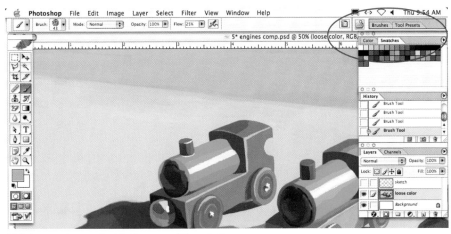

This is a workspace that I often use while painting.

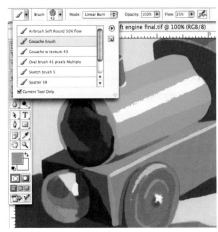

Choosing a Brush Tool preset

CUSTOMIZING YOUR PHOTOSHOP WORKSPACE

A custom workspace. Close the palettes that you won't need while painting and save your own palette layout by choosing Window > Workspace > Save Workspace.

Docking palettes. The palettes are designed to snap together to help you keep your workspace tidy. You can create your own combinations of palettes, for instance. Try

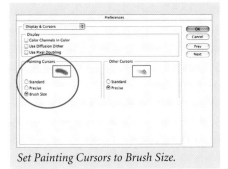

Smoother curves. When building custom brushes, make sure Smoothing is enabled in the Brushes palette. Smoothing helps create smoother curves in your brushstrokes and is most noticeable when you're painting quickly with a stylus.

dragging the Colors palette into the Layers palette group. You can dock frequently used palettes into the upper-right corner of the Options Bar.

Preferred Painting Cursors. You can set the painting cursors to display the shape of the brush tip at the size it's being used. Choose File > Photoshop Preferences > Display and Cursors. Set the Painting Cursors to Brush Size for most uses. When you're working with a tiny brush (just a few pixels), it can be difficult to see the tiny brush if you are not viewing using a high magnification. Then it's

Set Painting Cursors to Brush Size.

helpful to temporarily switch the painting cursor back to Standard.

Helpful Tool Presets. You can save your favorite brush presets as Tool Presets, located in the upper-left corner of the Options Bar. Choose the Brush tool, and select a brush preset from the Brushes palette that you'd like to save into the tool presets. Open the Tool Preset Picker, and then click the triangle to open its pop-up menu. Choose New Tool Preset, and then name and save your preset. It's helpful to save tool presets for the Eraser and other tools, as well.

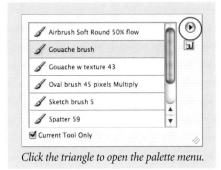

Click the triangle to open the palette menu.

Painter Basics for Artists

Instead of describing the details of every tool in Painter, this section focuses on the basics of Painter for artists who use a tablet. You'll find an overview of the interface, information about the Color palettes, Brush Selector Bar, Brush Creator and Brush Controls palettes, helpful tips for painters, and ideas for customizing your Painter workspace.

You'll begin with an overview of the Painter interface. The default Toolbox displays 14 tools. When you see an arrow in the lower right of a tool's field, click and hold, and the tools that are nested underneath the top tool will pop out. The Property Bar is a context-sensitive palette at the top of the screen that shows the settings for the current tool.

All of Painter's brushes are designed to work their best with a tablet. The brushes can express the nuances of your hand, including subtle movement—pressure, tilt, bearing angle (direction), and more.

 Saving your files. Save your working Painter files in RIFF format (Painter's native format) for the best performance and to preserve the program's native layers and effects, such as the "wet paint" and "impasto" paint.

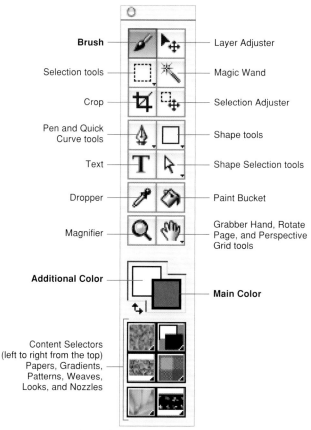

Brush — Layer Adjuster
Selection tools — Magic Wand
Crop — Selection Adjuster
Pen and Quick Curve tools — Shape tools
Text — Shape Selection tools
Dropper — Paint Bucket
Magnifier — Grabber Hand, Rotate Page, and Perspective Grid tools

Additional Color — Main Color

Content Selectors (left to right from the top) Papers, Gradients, Patterns, Weaves, Looks, and Nozzles

The Toolbox with emphasis on the painting, toning, and focus tools with controls that you can set up for a tablet

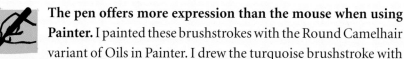 **The pen offers more expression than the mouse when using Painter.** I painted these brushstrokes with the Round Camelhair variant of Oils in Painter. I drew the turquoise brushstroke with a stylus and tablet and the purple stroke using a mouse.

THE PAINTER WORKSPACE

The Property Bar shows settings for the current tool

The Brush Selector Bar is where you choose Brush Categories and Brush Variants

Menu Bar

Toolbox

Content selectors

Colors palette

Mixer palette

Layers palette

Document window

Drawing mode icon

Navigation icon

Magnification slider

Two palette groups are docked on the right when you first launch Painter. The Colors palette displays a Hue Ring and Saturation/Value triangle that you can adjust to mix color. Nested with the Colors palette are the Mixer and Color Sets. With the Mixer, you can mix paint, just as you would on a traditional artist palette. Color Sets are useful for storing colors that you want to use

again. The second palette group includes the Layers and Channels palettes. The Layers palette allows you to store and manage elements that float above your image background. You can use the Channels palette to store your masks (alpha channels).

The magnification of the document is displayed in the lower-left corner of the Painter window. (100% magnification will display your image

with the most accuracy.) The Zoom slider lets you dynamically magnify or reduce your image.

Hide and show. Press the Tab key to hide or show the Toolbox and all of the palettes that are open.

Detail of Where All Creativity Comes From, *described in Chapter 14*

Using the Mix Color tool in the Mixer to make a new color

Helpful palettes. Use the Colors palette to choose color. Click in the Hue Ring to select a hue and mix tints and shades of the color using the Saturation/Value triangle. The Mixer palette* lets you mix color similar to how you would mix paint on a conventional artist's palette, whereas the Color Sets palette is a useful place to store your colors.

With the Layers palette, you can organize the elements in your paintings. Layers give you the flexibility to paint elements on their own layers, hide them, show them, and reposition them. For the image above, I painted colored washes on one layer, with the foreground washes and a drawing on layers above.

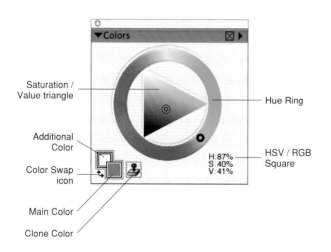

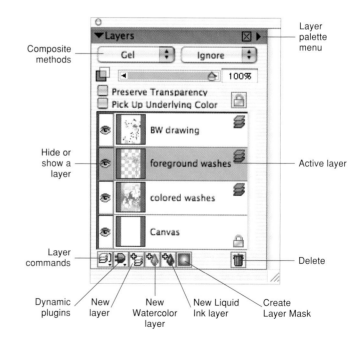

The Port du Val Cliffs and Beach at Etretat *in progress with Oil Pastels*

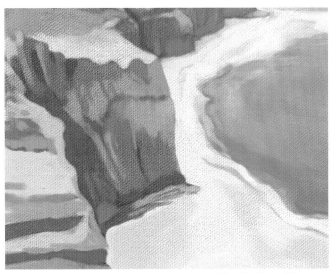

Downstream Path, Summer *in progress with Oils, Chalk, and Impasto*

The Brush Selector Bar. Painter ships with hundreds of exciting brushes. Use the Brush Selector Bar to choose brush categories and brush variants. To view the categories in List view, click the Brush Category icon to open the picker, and then click on the tiny triangle to the far right of the Brush Category menu to open the pop-out menu. To choose a new brush category, click on a name in the list. You can display the Brush Variant menu using the List view (shown here) or Stroke view. Click on a variant name to choose a brush. The triangle to the right of the Brush Variant icon opens a pop-up menu that allows you to choose a variant—in my case, the Chunky Oil Pastel 20.

Your own brush library. It's easy to create your own brush library that contains just the brush categories that you want. To begin, open the Brushes folder within the Painter application folder. Make a new folder and give it a name such as "My Brushes." Next, open the Painter Brushes folder and Alt/Option copy the brush categories that you want (and their jpegs) from the Painter Brushes folder into the "My Brushes" folder. To load your new library, choose Load library from the menu on the Brush Selector Bar, and choose your library in the Load Library dialog box.*

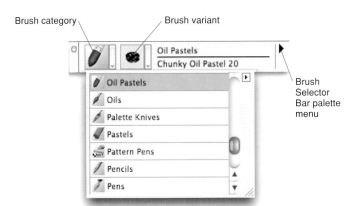

The Brush Selector Bar with the Brush Category menu shown in List view

LEARN MORE ABOUT. . .

* the Mixer. . . page 46
* using libraries. . . page 39

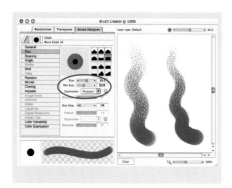

The Brush Creator and its Size section

Stroke drawn with the default Blunt Chalk

Stroke drawn with the custom Blunt Chalk

CUSTOMIZING BRUSHES

You can use the controls described here to create many of the custom brushes that are described in the projects later in this book.

The majority of Painter's brushes are already programmed to take advantage of a tablet. These exercises will help you understand what's going on "under the hood" so that you can customize brushes for your own personal feel. You can modify a default brush variant to change its stroke width and opacity based on the pressure you apply to the stylus. To try out the brush settings, begin by choosing the Brush tool in the Toolbox and opening the Brush Creator in Painter 8 or IX (Window > Show Brush Creator), or in Painter 6, 7, and IX, open the Brush Controls by choosing Window > Show Brush Controls. (If you're using the Brush Controls, you'll also need to open the General and Size sections.)

Choosing a brush and painting a stroke. In the Brush Selector Bar, choose the Chalk category and the Blunt Chalk variant. Apply varied pressure to your stylus while painting a squiggly brushstroke. You'll notice that the default brush reveals more grain when you apply less pressure.

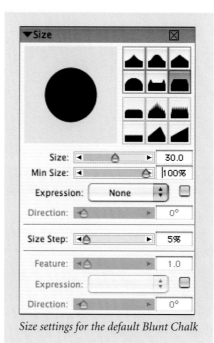

Size settings for the default Blunt Chalk

Setting the brush to change its stroke width. In the Size section (of the Brush Creator or Brush Controls), set the Min Size to 32%; then set the Expression pop-up menu to Pressure. Make another squiggly stroke, and you'll see the thickness of the stroke change based on the pressure that you apply to your stylus.

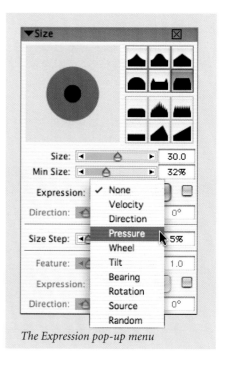

The Expression pop-up menu

The default Thick Bristle brushstroke

The custom Thick Bristle brushstroke

Detail of Downstream Path, Summer

More colorful brushstrokes. For this exercise, choose the Thick Bristle variant of Impasto. This brush (and others that use the same brush model) is actually a bundle of brush hairs, rather than a dab-based brush. You can load each hair with a different color. By default, the brush changes its opacity and stroke width based on the pressure that you apply to the stylus. Paint a stroke using the default Thick Bristle. By varying the pressure, you can achieve a sensitive range of opacity and stroke width. The bristles on this brush also

 More expression. You can set all of the Expression pop-up menus in the Brush Creator (and Brush Controls) to Velocity, Direction, Pressure, Wheel, Tilt, Bearing, Rotation, Source, and Random. (The Wheel operates with the airbrush pen fingerwheel.)

spread out based on the direction that you tilt the stylus.

Open the Color Variability section of the Brush Creator (or Brush Controls). Notice that the brush already has a small amount of Value variability built into it. Now set the Hue variability to about 15%, and then make a new brushstroke. You'll see subtle variation of color in the brush hairs.

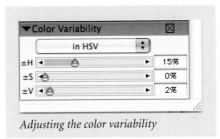

Adjusting the color variability

You'll find examples of variations of these brushes used in the projects in Chapters 8 and 12. In the *Distribudor, Old San Jose* painting, I painted textured strokes over oil paint using a Blunt Chalk. In *Downstream Path, Summer*, I used a Thick Bristle brush to add details of thick Impasto paint to the cliffs.

 Saving a brush category. To avoid losing custom brushes when you reset Painter to defaults or do a reinstall, it's a good idea to save your custom brushes into your own brush category. You must first choose an image that you want to use as an icon for the brush category. Open an image and make a 30-pixel square selection. From the pop-up menu on the Brush Selector Bar, choose Capture Brush Category, and give it a name. You'll find the brush you had chosen when you captured the icon in your new category. You can now copy brushes from other categories into your new container. It's a good idea to make a backup copy of your brush category. Painter IX users will find it in Users > Library > Application Support > Corel > Painter IX > Brushes > Painter Brushes. Those using earlier versions of Painter will find their new category within the Painter application folder > Brushes > Painter Brushes.

This is a palette layout that I often use while painting. Notice the custom oil pastel palette.

CUSTOMIZING YOUR PAINTER WORKSPACE

Painter has tools that allow you to set up your workspace for various kinds of projects. For instance, you can build a custom palette to store your brushes, tools, and commands. You can also create and save a palette layout for painting and a different one for compositing that might include the Layers and Channels palettes. Additionally, you can create new brush categories,* and import alternative brush and art material libraries into the program.

LEARN MORE ABOUT. . .

* your own brush library. . . page 35

* new brush categories. . . page 37

Making your own custom palettes. For the *Etretat* study above, I created a custom palette to hold my oil pastels and papers. To create your own custom palette, choose a brush variant (I chose the Chunky Oil Pastel 20), and drag it from the Brush Selector Bar. A small palette with the brush will automatically appear. Drag the lower-right corner to expand the size of the palette. Choose another variant and drag and drop it onto the palette. To add a paper texture, drag a paper texture from the Paper Selector or the Papers palette onto your palette. To save and name your palette using the Organizer, choose Window > Custom Palette > Organizer, and enter a name for your palette.

Saving a custom palette layout. For more intuitive painting, it's helpful to simplify your workspace by closing palettes that you don't need while painting. If you're not using layers, you might need only the Colors palette and the Mixer. In this illustration, I have opened the Size section of the Brush Controls in Painter IX because it gives me useful information about the size of the brush, its Brush Tip Profile, the Expression pop-up menu, and more. (The Brush Controls palette is also available in Painter 6 and 7.) To save a custom layout, choose Window > Arrange Palettes > Save Layout. Name your layout in the New Palette Layout dialog box and click OK.

In this detail of Distribudor, *you can see the grainy chalk strokes overlaid on top of the oil paint.*

Useful brush cursors. To specify a Brush Cursor type and to set the orientation of the cursor, choose Corel Painter > Preferences > General (Mac OS X) or Edit > Preferences > Brush Tracking (Windows). (I prefer using a Triangle when Brush Ghost is not enabled.)

In this chapter, you learned about setting up your tablet and artists' basics for Painter and Photoshop. In the next chapter, you'll work with more brushes and paint.

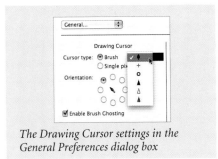

The Drawing Cursor settings in the General Preferences dialog box

 Using libraries. Libraries are containers that hold the brushes, paper textures, and other items that you can create using Painter. Movers let you customize these containers by transferring items into or out of them. For a more detailed explanation of how movers and libraries work, see *The Painter Wow! Book* or the Painter documentation. Every palette that has a resource list of materials has an Open Library (or Load Library) command. Let's use the Brush Selector Bar as an example. Choose Window > Show Brush Selector. (If you have Painter 6 or 7, open the Brushes palette.) Open the palette pop-up menu, and choose Load Brush Library to

display a dialog box that lets you search through folders on your hard disk until you find the library you want. Then double-click to open it. (Although you can load libraries directly from a CD-ROM—like the Painter IX CD-ROM or the *Painter Wow! Book* CD-ROM, it's more reliable to copy the libraries from the CD-ROM into your Painter application folder.)

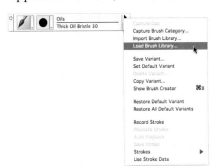

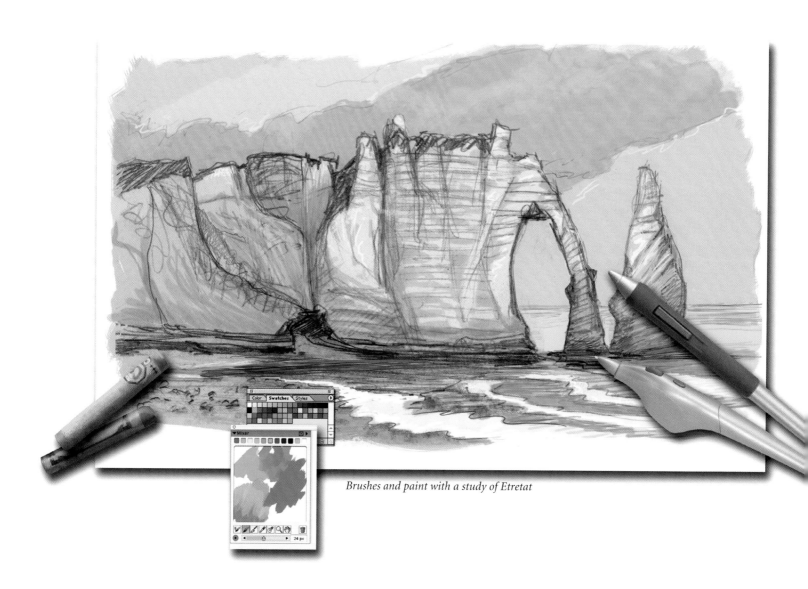

Brushes and paint with a study of Etretat

3

ASSEMBLING BRUSHES AND PAINT

The first part of this chapter focuses on the process of assembling your brushes and paint, and mixing colors. Then you'll explore some exciting brushes in both Photoshop and Painter. You'll gain experience with using the default brushes, combined with a pressure-sensitive tablet, and discover the unique capabilities of each brush. This experience will be helpful when you work through the drawing and painting projects in the following chapters, and also when you create the custom brushes in later chapters.

 Now you'll pick up your stylus, mix paint, and have fun exploring the brushes. My favorite Wacom 6 x 8 Intuos pressure-sensitive tablet used in combination with the brushes in Photoshop and Painter allows for creativity and control when painting a wide variety of brushstrokes. For this chapter I chose to use default brushes that are easy to use in each program. Each program offers unique brush features. For instance, Photoshop offers a variety of brushes that respond to pressure or to the tilt of the stylus (such as the Airbrush 75 Tilt Angle), which paints a thick to thin stroke as you tilt the stylus as you draw; Painter offers its own unique brushes that respond to pressure, tilt, and the rotation of your hand as you draw. For instance, the Bristle Oils brush allows you to spread the bristles of the brush as you tilt the stylus or while you make a curved stroke. I hope you enjoy your exploration.

Exploring Brushes and Paint in Photoshop

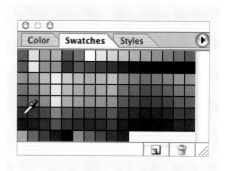

Selecting a dark red from the Swatches palette

Continued on page 44

1 Setting up. In this exercise, you'll explore using some of the default brushes in Photoshop with your tablet and stylus. First, you'll need to set up a new file and choose a color in preparation for experimenting with the brushes. Make a new file that measures 600 x 600 pixels. (I suggest using the same size file for all of these exercises.) In the Color Mode pop-up menu, choose RGB Color.

The New dialog box set up for the file

LEARN MORE ABOUT. . .

* choosing colors. . . page 26

* the Brushes palette. . . page 27

2 Choosing paint color. Now choose a dark red from the Swatches palette (Window > Swatches).

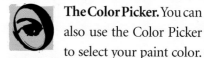 **The Color Picker.** You can also use the Color Picker to select your paint color. To display the Color Picker, click the Foreground Color in the Toolbox. To choose a hue, click in the vertical bar. To make the color less saturated, click on the left side of the Select Foreground Color field. To give your color more saturation, click on the right side of the field. To darken the color, click lower in the field; to lighten it, move higher.

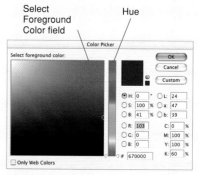

The dark red shown in the Color Picker

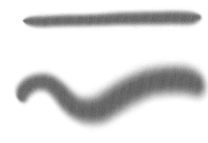

Hard Round 19 pixels, scaled to 60 pixels

Soft Round 65 pixels

Airbrush 75 Tilt Angle

3 **Drawing thin-to-thick strokes with hard edges.** Choose the Brush tool in the Toolbox, and then open the Brushes palette (Window > Brushes).* Click the triangle on the Brushes tab, and then choose Small List (which will allow you to see a small picture of the brush dab and its name). Now click on Brush Presets and scroll to choose the Hard Round 19 pixels preset.

Press lightly on your stylus, and gradually increase pressure as you draw a horizontal line. Now draw a wiggly line that varies in thickness based on the pressure applied.

4 **Drawing thin-to-thick strokes with soft edges.** Choose the Soft Round 65 pixels preset, and apply light pressure for a thin stroke and heavier pressure for a heavier stroke.

 Adjusting spacing. When I increased the size of the Hard Round 19 pixels preset, my brushstroke had rough edges because the dabs did not overlap sufficiently to make a smooth-edged stroke. To give the brush smooth edges, I decreased the spacing between the dabs of paint. Click on Brush Tip Shape and increase the diameter of the brush to 60 pixels; then decrease the spacing to make the dabs overlap. Experiment with the spacing of your brush. (I chose 15%.) Overly tight spacing can cause slower performance.

5 **Making strokes that vary with tilt.** Now choose the Airbrush 75 Tilt Angle preset. Hold the stylus upright and draw a horizontal line. Next, tilt the stylus as you draw a wavy line. Notice that the stroke thickness increases with more tilt.

Top stroke rough; bottom stroke smooth

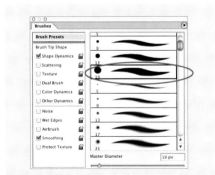

The Hard Round 19 pixels preset is chosen.

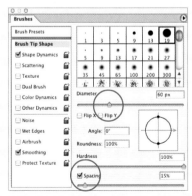

Adjusting the Spacing slider for the brush

Airbrush Pen Opacity Flow   *Rough Round Bristle*

6 Making strokes with varied opacity. Now choose the Airbrush Pen Opacity Flow preset. Press lightly on your stylus and gradually increase pressure as you draw a horizontal line. Now draw a curved line that varies in opacity based on the pressure applied.

 Loading brushes. Photoshop ships with several additional groups of brushes, and it's easy to load them into your Brushes palette. Click the arrow on the top right of the Brushes palette to access the pop-out menu, and look near the bottom of its list. Choose one of the libraries. After making your choice, you'll see a dialog box that asks whether you want to "replace the current brushes" with the new library you've chosen (click OK) or add the new brush set to your list (click Append).

7 Painting thin-to-thick strokes with varied edges. Choose the Rough Round Bristle preset, and apply light pressure for a thin stroke with smooth edges. For a thicker stroke with rougher edges, apply heavier pressure.

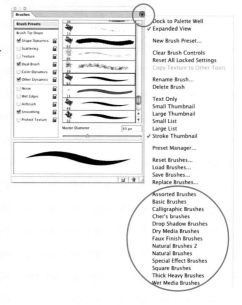

Watercolor Loaded Wet Flat Tip

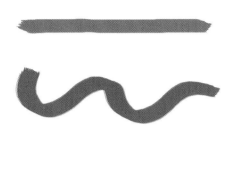
Chalk 60

Charcoal Large Smear

8 Painting with flat brushes. The Watercolor Loaded Wet Flat Tip preset has a flat tip. Press lightly on your stylus, and gradually increase pressure as you draw a translucent horizontal line. Now draw a wiggly line that varies in thickness based on pressure applied. You'll notice that the thickness of the stroke also changes based on the orientation of the stylus. Then draw a stroke that overlaps an existing stroke, and notice the transparency of the paint.*

Next, choose the Chalk 60 preset. Press lightly on your stylus, and gradually increase pressure as you draw an opaque horizontal line. Now draw a wiggly line that varies in thickness based on the pressure applied. You will notice that the thickness of the stroke also changes based on the orientation of the stylus.

The Charcoal Large Smear preset also has a rectangular tip. Choose it in the Brushes palette. Press lightly on your stylus, and gradually

increase pressure as you draw a horizontal line. Notice how the opacity increases as you apply more pressure. Now draw a wiggly line that varies in thickness based on the pressure applied. You'll notice that the thickness of the stroke also subtly changes based on how the stylus is rotated in your hand as you draw. Now make a few smaller strokes that overlap. New paint builds up nicely on top of existing paint.

LEARN MORE ABOUT. . .

* opacity and pressure. . . pages 29, 171
* transparent paint. . . pages 108–111, 201

Exploring Brushes and Paint in Painter

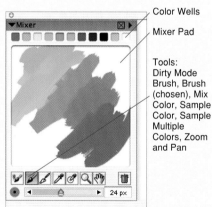

Choosing a nice medium-blue in the Colors palette

ARTIST'S MATERIALS

Tablet: Light to medium pressure (set in the Tip Control Panel)

Program: Painter

Paint: Choose a blue color in the Colors palette (H 90, S 44, V 50 is shown here), mix a blue using the Mixer or type these RGB values into Color Info; R 73, G 138, B 187

Paper Texture: Basic Paper

Brushes:

• Grainy Variable Pencil: stroke changes depending on the tilt and angle of the stylus

• Square X-Soft Pastel: stroke changes depending on the tilt and angle of the stylus; texture changes with pressure applied

• Round Camelhair: stroke changes in thickness and opacity with pressure

Continued on page 48

1 **Setting up.** Now you'll explore some of Painter's brushes using a tablet and stylus. Begin by making a new file that measures 600 x 600 pixels. (I suggest using the same size file for all of these exercises.) Then set Brush Tracking so that you can customize Painter to the nuances of your hand on the stylus and tablet.*

The Mixer. You can mix color on-the-fly using the Mixer. (If the Mixer is not open, choose Window > Show Mixer.) You can choose a color from the Swatches or from the Colors palette and apply it to the Mixer Pad using your stylus and the Brush tool in the Mixer. Blend the colors with one another using the Mix Color tool, just as you would on a traditional artist's palette. The Dirty Mode Brush allows the Brush tool to smear new color with color already on the pad. To adjust the size of the Mixer's Brush or Mix Color tools, use the slider at the bottom of the palette. Increase the size of the Brush tool to 30 pixels and add a new color to a painted area. You'll notice that the smeariness of the Brush tool and character of the stroke are affected by how you brush over existing color with your stylus.

2 **Choosing paint color.** Next, choose a medium-blue color in the Colors palette (Window > Show Colors). Click in the round Hue Ring to select a hue; then click in the Saturation/Value triangle to lighten, darken, or adjust the saturation of the color. You can also create paint color using the Mixer.*

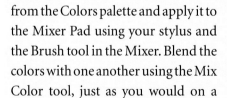

Grainy Variable Pencil strokes, painted while varying the angle and direction of the stylus

Square X-Soft Pastel strokes, painted with lesser pressure applied at the beginning of strokes

Round Camelhair strokes, painted with lesser pressure applied at the beginning of strokes

3 Drawing with pencils. The Grainy Variable Pencil is sensitive to the angle, direction, and pressure of the stylus as you draw. Choose the Pencils category and the Grainy Variable Pencil variant. Hold the stylus comfortably in your hand. Now draw a wavy line and vary the tilt and the pressure on the stylus as you draw a line. The character of the line will change as you make variations in pressure, as well as subtle hand and wrist movements, such as the angle of the pen changing as you draw. Experiment with other variants in the Pencils category.

4 Brushstrokes with texture. Brushes with the word "grainy" in their name will paint a grain-sensitive stroke. Others will reveal texture based on their traditional counterparts, such as the Chalk and Pastels categories. Choose the Square X-Soft Pastel 30 variant of Pastels. Hold the stylus comfortably in your hand, draw a wavy line, and vary the angle and the pressure of the stylus. The stroke will change as you vary the pressure and the angle of the pen as you draw. Applying less pressure will reveal more texture.

5 Painting brushstrokes of varied width and opacity. For a brushstroke with varied thickness, try the Round Camelhair variant of Oils. Begin your stroke by pressing lightly on the stylus and then gradually building up pressure. If you've carefully controlled the pressure, you'll notice that your stroke gradually expanded in width from thin to thick, depending on the pressure you've applied.

Choosing the Grainy Variable Pencil

LEARN MORE ABOUT. . .

* Brush Tracking. . . page 52
* the Mixer. . . page 46
* the Papers palette. . . page 35

Revealing texture. When you draw with a texture-sensitive brush (such as the Grainy Variable Pencil), the texture will be revealed in the stroke as you draw. (When you boot Painter, a texture is loaded automatically.) You can choose a new texture by clicking the Paper Selector in the Toolbox and then choosing from the pop-out menu.

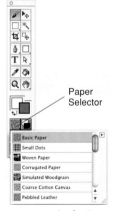

Paper Selector

Choosing a paper texture in the Paper Selector

Flat Oils strokes drawn with stylus held at more of an angle

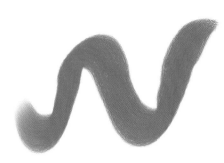

Flat Oils stroke drawn with stylus rotated in hand while drawing

ARTIST'S MATERIALS

Brushes:

• Flat Oils: stroke width changes with orientation of stylus

• Thick Bristle Oils: bristles spread out depending on the angle of the stylus

• Fine Spray Airbrush: spray pattern and stroke width change with angle of stylus

6 Painting thick and thin strokes with flat brushes. With the flat brushes, you can paint wide or narrow strokes, depending on the way you hold the stylus, and the pressure that you apply. When practicing the strokes that follow, position your stylus with the button between your index finger and thumb (toward the left if you are right-handed, or toward the right if you are left-handed). With the Brush tool chosen in the Toolbox, choose the Flat Oils 30 variant of Oils from the Brush Selector Bar. To paint a thick horizontal stroke, pull the brush straight across your image using even pressure. To make thin lines, pull down. To make a wavy line of varied thickness, use light pressure on your stylus for the beginning of the stroke, and more pressure as you sweep up and rotate the brush to come back down.

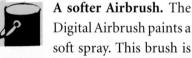 **A softer Airbrush.** The Digital Airbrush paints a soft spray. This brush is useful for subtle touch-up work, but the spray pattern does not change when you hold the stylus with an angle, as it does with the continuous stroke Airbrushes such as the Fine Spray described in step 8. The Tapered Detail Air and Soft Airbrush are also "soft" airbrushes.

LEARN MORE ABOUT. . .

* the Airbrushes. . . page 49
* continuous stroke model. . . page 48
* Color Variability. . . page 37

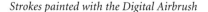

Strokes painted with the Digital Airbrush

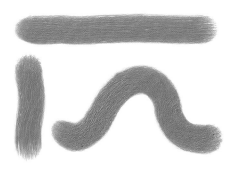

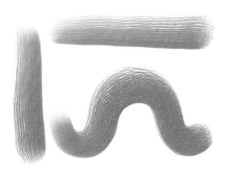

Thick Bristle Oils strokes, painted with stylus held nearly upright

Thick Bristle Oils strokes, drawn with stylus held at more of an angle

Fine Spray Airbrush strokes painted with stylus held at various angles

7 Making bristles spread. For a brush that spreads its bristles as it applies thick paint (depending on how you hold the stylus), choose the Oils category from the Brush Selector Bar, and then choose the Thick Oil Bristle 30 variant. Hold your stylus as upright as you can, and draw a stroke. Notice the bristle edges at the beginning and end of the stroke and

the thick paint texture. Next, hold the stylus in a more natural, slightly angled position (with the top of the pen tilted toward you), and draw a second stroke. See how the bristles on the top of the second stroke appear to splay, or spread out, just the way a conventional brush does when you press it down and pull a stroke across your canvas?

8 Painting with Airbrushes. The Fine Spray variant of Airbrushes allows you to spray paint just like a traditional airbrush. Hold the stylus vertically in your hand, and paint a horizontal stroke. Now hold the stylus comfortably in your hand in a more angled position, and paint a stroke. See how the paint sprays farther out across the canvas; the more you angle the stylus, the farther the brush will spray. Other Airbrushes (such as the Coarse Spray) also allow this kind of control.

In this chapter, you've learned how to set up your brushes and paint and you've experimented with brushes. Now you're ready for the tablet and drawing exercises in the next chapter.

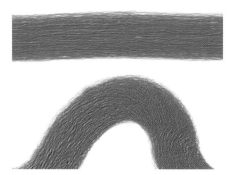

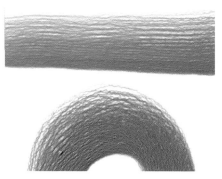

Close-up view of the Thick Bristle Oil bristles, stylus upright

Close-up view of the Thick Bristle Oil bristles, stylus held at an angle

California Pottery Fish: *Gesture, clean line, modified contour, and sketchy line styles of drawing*

4

DRAWING AND TABLET EXERCISES

In this chapter, you'll begin by choosing a subject and setting up a still life. Then you'll do exercises that will help loosen up your hand and help you to build control using the tablet and stylus. Next, you will use four different drawing methods (or ways of seeing) to sketch the subject: gesture, contour, clean line, and sketchy line. The objective is not to draw photo-realistic illustrations, but to draw with sensitivity and expression. After completing these exercises, you will intimately know your subject.

To simulate the look of various graphite pencils, I drew these drawings using a dark gray. I drew the California Pottery Fish *illustrations using Painter and my favorite Wacom 6 x 8 Intuos tablet and pen. The pressure-sensitive tablet used in combination with the great variety of brushes in Painter allowed me to have control and expression while drawing different kinds of lines. For the subject, I chose a favorite ceramic pottery fish, and placed it on a light-colored surface. I lit the fish using a small spotlight, which I positioned behind and to the left of the subject. Prior to beginning the drawings, I carefully studied the forms and space around the fish, which were enhanced by the lighting. Then I relaxed and used a sensitive hand while drawing. I use one or more of these drawing methods as I'm warming up before a painting session.*

Warming Up and Sketching

A digital photo of the subject

The artist with still life set up and computer

1 **Setting up a still life.** Choose a simple ceramic figure, or a cup or vase and set up your still life on a light-colored surface. I chose this fish as a subject because of its graceful flowing curves, and the interesting simple forms. The shape of the fish and the negative space around it are intriguing.

Choose a small spotlight that will cast interesting shadows on the table surface. After my still life was set up, I photographed it with a digital camera so I could save it as a reference for readers of this chapter.*

When practicing the exercises that follow, remember to relax and enjoy the drawing process. The computer is forgiving—you can "undo" a line if you don't like it—or start over in a new file without wasting a precious sheet of expensive drawing paper.

2 **Practicing warm-up exercises.** Before beginning to sketch your subject, perform the following exercises to loosen up your drawing hand and to get comfortable with your tablet and stylus.*

You'll begin each of the warm-up exercises with a new 600 x 600 pixel file (File > New). In the Colors palette, choose a dark gray color for sketching. I suggest using the same dark gray for all of the exercises.

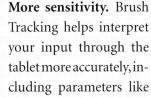

More sensitivity. Brush Tracking helps interpret your input through the tablet more accurately, including parameters like pressure and speed. Choose Preferences, Brush Tracking, and make a single stroke in the window that varies from soft to hard pressure, including slow to fast movement. The speed is essential for accurate input while doing quick gesture drawings.

PHOTOGRAPH: MELINDA HOLDEN

The artist's hand on the tablet

Circles: Grainy Variable Pencil

Square: 2B Pencil

3 **Drawing loose circles.** For the circle exercise, choose the Brush tool in the Toolbox, and the 2B Pencil variant of Pencils from the Brush Selector Bar. Place your tablet in a comfortable position on the table near you, or on your lap if your tablet is a 6 X 8 size. Hold your stylus comfortably in

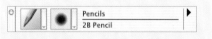

The Brush Selector Bar with the 2B variant of Pencils chosen

your hand, as you would a pen or pencil when writing. Move your hand in a circular motion a few inches above your tablet, in a way that feels natural and smooth. Now that you have the motion, touch your stylus to your tablet using medium pressure, and rotate your hand and stylus in a circular motion. Bear down harder on one side of the circle than the other, and notice how the stroke darkens with the heavier pressure.

4 **Sketching a square.** Now choose the 2B Pencil variant of Pencils, and sketch a square. Begin the square by applying a medium pressure and drawing a horizontal line. Using a similar pressure, draw a second horizontal line, lower in the image, parallel to the first. Position your stylus on the left edge of the top line, and pull down using medium pressure on the stylus, drawing a vertical line. Draw a second vertical line to finish the right side of the square.

Drawing cursor. You'll be using Pencils variants with small tips for this project, so it's a good idea to set the Preferences for the Drawing Cursor to show the Brush cursor at all times. This cursor is easier to see as you're drawing with a fine pencil than when using the Brush Ghost.* Under the Corel Painter 8 menu, choose Preferences > General (Mac) / Edit > Preferences > General (PC) > and set the Drawing Cursor to Brush. Make sure to uncheck the Enable Brush Ghost check box. Click OK to close the Preferences dialog box.

The Brush Ghost for the Flattened Pencil (left) and the Brush cursor (right)

The Preferences > General dialog box showing the Drawing Cursor setup

LEARN MORE ABOUT. . .

* the Brush Ghost. . . pages 39, 53
* Brush Tracking. . . page 52
* the Colors palette. . . pages 34, 46, 102

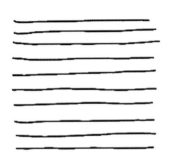

Horizontal Lines: Mechanical Pencil 1.5

Ringlet Squiggles: Flattened Pencil

A quick gesture drawing of the fish

5 **Drawing parallel lines.** Now you'll practice developing more control when using consistent pressure while drawing a set of horizontal lines. Choose the Mechanical Pencil 1.5 variant of Pencils. Position your wrist on your tablet to support your hand and allow more control while drawing the lines. Try experimenting with holding your stylus more erect for this exercise. Press the stylus firmly on the tablet and use careful, consistent pressure while drawing the first horizontal line. Then draw several more lines under the first using the same consistent pressure.

6 **Drawing squiggles.** Next, you'll use the Flattened Pencil to sketch a series of loose ringlets. Choose the Flattened Pencil variant of Pencils and draw a series of curved ringlet lines. Press lightly on your tablet, and then use heavier pressure. Allow your hand to rotate naturally while drawing the lines. The Flattened Pencil is sensitive to pressure, as well as the angle you hold the stylus while drawing. This added expression contributes to a satisfying artist experience.

Open a new file—I recommend using the same size file for the remainder of the exercises. My file measured 1500 X 2000 pixels.

7 **Drawing a gesture.** A gesture is drawn quickly and loosely— it captures the movement and energy of a subject. Gestures are often drawn of people and other living things. Although the ceramic fish is an inanimate object, it has beautiful flowing curves, which make it an ideal subject for gesture. Choose the Grainy Variable Pencil variant of Pencils. Carefully observe your subject, and let your eyes sweep around its forms.

Press your stylus firmly on your tablet and sketch a movement gesture of your subject with fast, loose strokes. Experiment with varying the pressure while sketching. Focus on quickly sketching the essence of your subject in just a few seconds. You might want to repeat this exercise several times to become better acquainted with your subject.

For Photoshop users. If you don't have Painter, you can follow along with these exercises in Photoshop using the Dry Media Brushes. See the instructional sidebar on page 57 for how to load these brushes. Use the #2 Pencil for steps 1–8. Try the Charcoal Pencil for steps 9 and 10. (Although they're useful, the performance of the brushes will not be identical.)

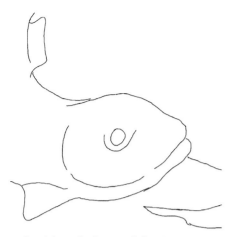
A detail from the "contour" drawing

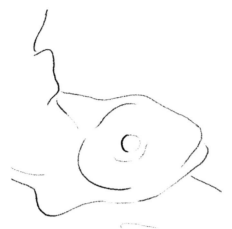
A detail from the modified contour drawing

The "sketchy line" style is shown in this detail.

8 Drawing a contour. A contour drawing is a sensitive, careful drawing style that usually shows the edges of forms in space. During this exercise, you'll imagine that your stylus is actually moving along the edges of the subject, and draw using a controlled, consistent line. This exercise will help you to develop more control over the pressure that you exert on the tablet. Choose the Mechanical Pencil 1.5 variant of Pencils. This pencil will allow you to draw a line of even thickness and value, provided that you apply a consistent pressure to the tablet. Carefully observe your subject. To achieve a consistent line, apply pressure to the pen on the tablet as evenly as possible. Let your hand move in a controlled manner as you draw. See if you can draw around the outside of the subject without lifting your stylus from the tablet (as you would your pencil from the paper).

9 Making a modified contour. This adaptation of the contour method will allow you to be more expressive with the line quality. Making a modified contour drawing will help you to become more sensitive and observant while becoming more intimate with your subject. You'll also develop more control over varied pressure using your stylus and tablet. Choose the Thick and Thin Pencil. Touch the stylus to your tablet, and let your eye follow the edges of the forms as you draw. Vary the pressure as you draw an indented area of a form. In an area where you see a highlight or a raised form, decrease your pressure slightly, so that the strength and opacity of the line vary in an expressive way. Pretend that you are tracing around the edges of the forms with your stylus. If you like, add a few important internal contours.

10 Using a sketchy line style. This kind of line is composed of multiple overlapping strokes (hence its name). Take the time to study your subject carefully and analyze its basic forms and shapes. Think about how you can simplify the subject so that in the beginning, you draw just the basic shapes using loose strokes. Using the 2B Pencil, apply light pressure to your stylus as you rough in the basic shapes. Don't draw a continuous line around your subject. Instead, sketch in a way similar to how you would use a pencil, with sketchy lines that overlap one another to suggest the curves and straighter lines. As you begin to refine the edges of your drawing, embellish the most important areas by applying heavier pressure to create bolder marks. (Apply heavier pressure, and then let up gradually as you come out of a curve, for instance.) Congratulations! You've completed the drawing exercises. An instructional sidebar follows.

Sketching in Photoshop

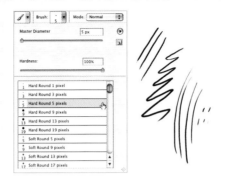

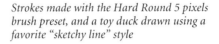

Strokes made with the Hard Round 5 pixels brush preset, and a toy duck drawn using a favorite "sketchy line" style

Artists who love responsiveness while doing quick sketches will enjoy many of Photoshop's simpler brush presets. (Simple means "no performance-hungry settings in the Brush palette, like the Dual Brush setting.") In the first example, you'll use a brush that is ideal for drawing lines similar to a round-tipped ink pen or pencil. For the second example, you will load a brush that will allow you to draw lines of variable thickness based on the angle you hold the stylus.

Setting up for drawing. Create a new file that measures 1500 x 2000 pixels. (All of the examples presented in this sidebar use the same size file.) Choose a dark gray in the Color Picker (to simulate graphite). Now choose the Brush tool in the Toolbox. In preparation for the second drawing example, load the Calligraphic Brushes as follows: Choose the Brush tool; then click on the tiny arrow on the top right of the Brushes palette and, when the menu pops open, choose the Calligraphic Brushes from near the bottom of the list. A dialog box will appear asking "Replace current brushes with the brushes from the Calligraphic set?" Click the Append button to add them to your existing Brushes palette.

Drawing with a "sketchy line." For the first toy duck sketch, I used the "sketchy line" method, in which the strokes gently overlap one another, to create curves and to render straighter lines. This type of drawing has an energetic, airy approach, and it is forgiving because you build up areas of emphasis gradually.

Photoshop's Hard Round 5 pixels brush preset is ideal for drawing smooth lines with crisp edges, and for the technique that follows. Choose the Brush tool in the Toolbox; then open the Brushes palette (Window > Brushes). Click the triangle on the Brushes tab and choose Small List (which allows you to see a small picture of the brush dab and its name). Now click on Brush Presets and scroll to choose the Hard Round 5 pixels preset.

I suggest making a few practice marks to get to know your brush. This brush is already set up to vary opacity and stroke width with pressure, so to achieve a darker line, press harder with your stylus, and to draw a lighter line, apply lighter pressure. While drawing, avoid doing any erasing, because building up layers of line work adds character to your drawing. When you sketch a line, begin with a lighter pressure and, if you like the line, sketch over it again to emphasize it. Above all, relax and enjoy the drawing process.

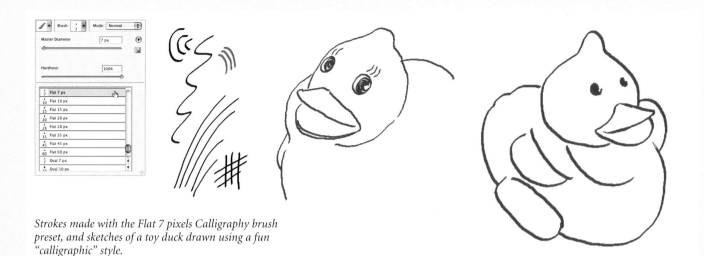

Strokes made with the Flat 7 pixels Calligraphy brush preset, and sketches of a toy duck drawn using a fun "calligraphic" style.

Drawing with a "calligraphic" line. For the second sketch, you'll use a flat brush that draws lines of varying thickness depending on the angle of the stylus—a "calligraphic line"—to create a simple modified contour that focuses on the edges of the subject.

Begin by creating a new file and choose the Flat 7 pixels brush that was imported when you loaded the Calligraphic Brushes set earlier. Click on the little arrow to the right of the brush tip preview in the Options Bar to pop out the Brush Preset Picker; then choose the Flat 7 pixels preset from the list. (You can also choose the brush from the Brush Preset list in the Brushes palette.) Make some practice marks and notice how the line varies if you start a stroke from the right or the left and pull up or down.

Observe your subject, and imagine tracing your stylus around the edge of the forms. To steady your hand while using this controlled drawing method, place your forearm or the base of your hand on the edge of the table and hold your stylus as you would a writing pen. Touch your stylus to the tablet and begin drawing. Don't worry if your lines wiggle a little; it will add to the hand-drawn look.

I hope you've enjoyed this exercise. Now you're ready to move on to learning about volume in Chapter 5, "The Illusion of Volume."

Loading more Photoshop brushes. In Photoshop's Dry Media Brushes, you'll find the #2 Pencil, which is a great brush for doing methodical drawings (such as the contour method described on page 55), but if you sketch quickly as I do, the performance can lag. To load the Dry Media Brushes, choose the Brush tool; then click on the tiny arrow on the top right of the Brushes palette. When the menu opens, choose the Dry Media Brushes from near the bottom of the list. A dialog box appears, asking if you'd like to Append or Replace the brushes with the new set. Choose Append to add them to your existing Brushes palette.

To learn how to make my "sketcher" brush with which you can sketch quickly and with good performance while revealing texture, turn to pages 116 and 117 in Chapter 9, "Making Brushes for Sketching and Painting."

LEARN MORE ABOUT. . .

* the "Sketchy line" method. . . page 56
* the "Contour" method. . . page 55

Vintage Bauer pitcher

5

The Illusion of Volume

To begin, you'll draw a cube and an orange, which will help you to understand how to model solid objects. After the cube and orange, there is a sidebar that features modeling using Photoshop. After completing these exercises, you'll set up a still life using a more complex object and paint it so that it has volume, weight, and mass.

It's helpful to practice the process of modeling form in a monochromatic painting before moving on to using both color and value together, because the composition of a color painting will not hold up without well thought-out values.

I drew the cube, the orange, and the pitcher using my Wacom tablet and stylus. The pressure-sensitive tablet used in combination with the Pastels brushes in Painter allowed me to have control while drawing the lines and shaded areas. For a more complex subject, I chose a blue ring-ware pitcher and placed it on a light-colored tabletop near my computer. I lit the pitcher using a small lamp, which I positioned to the upper left of the subject. Prior to beginning the drawing, I carefully studied the forms and space around the pitcher, which were enhanced by the lighting.

My objective was to create an interpretive drawing, but not a photo-realistic rendering. I purposely simplified forms and sometimes slightly distorted them to enhance the composition. Also, I added a horizon line and painted a graduated background to give depth and interest to the image.

Sketching a Cube

Sharp Pastel Pencil, *varied pressure*

Square Hard Pastel, *light pressure*

Square Hard Pastel, *heavier pressure*

The sketched diamond shape

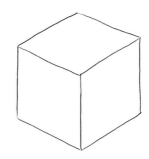

The line drawing of the cube

ARTIST'S MATERIALS

Tablet: Medium pressure

Program: Painter

Paper: Sketchbook Paper: crisp, medium-grain texture

Paint: Dark gray, chosen in the Colors palette

Brushes:

• Sharp Pastel Pencil: ideal for sketching, reveals texture, and produces an expressive line that varies with pressure

• Square Hard Pastel: allows subtle building of values while revealing paper texture; heavier pressure also creates a varied texture effect

1 **Warm-up: A solid cube.** This exercise will help you understand the concept of volume and solidity of a form in space. If you are familiar with the concept, you can skip step 1 and move on to step 2.

You'll draw a cube that is lit from the upper left. Imagine a "solid" cube—one that is cut from granite. Thinking of it as a heavy, solid cube will help you to draw it as one.

You'll begin the exercise with a new 600 x 600 pixel file. In the Colors palette, choose a dark gray.* In the Paper Selector (Toolbox), select the Sketchbook Paper texture.*

Choose the Sharp Pastel Pencil variant of Pastels from the Brush Selector Bar. Next, I recommend setting Brush Tracking so that Painter can customize itself to the pressure and speed of your hand on the stylus and tablet.* You'll start the cube by drawing a diamond shape. Now sketch an angled line. Add a second

line, parallel to the first. Draw two more angled lines that connect the first two. Try to maintain an even pressure on the stylus so that all of the lines are a similar shade of gray.

To sketch the sides of the cube, draw three vertical lines. For the bottom of the cube, draw two diagonal lines that connect the bottom of the vertical lines. I used Painter's Page Rotation tool to rotate the image, which made it easier to draw the straight, angled lines.*

LEARN MORE ABOUT...

* using the Colors palette. . . pages 46, 102
* using the Paper Selector. . . pages 32, 180
* Brush Tracking. . . page 52
* Page Rotation tool. . . page 32
* shading and value. . . page 64

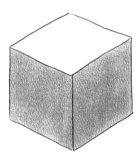

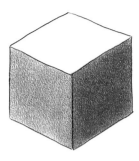

The cube sketch partially shaded

Suggesting a light source by adding shading

The final cube with cast shadow added

2 Shading the cube. Adding tone to the sides of the cube will help to suggest volume. Envision a light source shining from the top left.

Now you'll use the same gray that you chose for the lines to add shading to two sides of your cube. Choose the Square Hard Pastel variant of Pastels from the Brush Selector Bar. Use a light pressure on your stylus, and build up the shading for an even coverage on the two side planes. Aim for a medium-gray value.*

Tone and value. Tone (or value) is the lightness or darkness given to a surface by the amount of light reflected from it. Black in the shadow areas is the darkest value, and white in the highlights is the lightest value.

3 Building up darker shading. To emphasize the light source shining from the upper left, use soft, controlled strokes to build up darker shading in the right side of the cube.

Page Rotation. With the Page Rotation tool, you can rotate the image to a comfortable drawing position, which makes it easier to sketch angled lines. Press the Grabber Hand tool to pop out the Page Rotation tool (Space-Alt/Option-Drag). Click and drag with the tool on your image to rotate it. To return the image to its original position, double-click on the Page Rotation tool in the Toolbox.

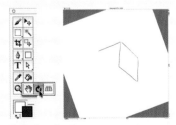

Rotating the page

4 Adding a cast shadow. A cast shadow will help to place your cube on a surface and add to the illusion of space, and its volume or weight. Draw your cast shadow darker as you get closer to the edge of the cube, and let it gradually fade out at its outer edge.

For Photoshop users. If you don't have Painter, you can follow along with these exercises in Photoshop using the Dry Media Brushes. See the instructional sidebar on page 57 on how to load the brushes. Use the Charcoal Pencil for the cube. For the orange on page 62, try the Pastel on Charcoal Paper. For the pitcher, try the Pastel Rough Texture and the Soft Pastel Large. (Although they're useful, the performance of the brushes will not be identical.)

Drawing a Textured Round Object

Sharp Pastel Pencil, *varied pressure*

Square Hard Pastel, *light pressure*

Square Hard Pastel, *heavier pressure*

The sketched outline of the orange

The orange partially shaded with medium gray

ARTIST'S MATERIAL

Tablet: medium-soft pressure

Program: Painter

Paint: Grays chosen in the Colors palette

Paper: "Basic Paper," versatile medium-grain texture

Brushes:

- "Soft Pastel Pencil," ideal for sketching, both texture and opacity vary with pressure

- "Square X-Soft Pastel," allows subtle building of values, while revealing paper texture; stroke width varies slightly with the angle of stylus

1 **Warm-up: A round object.** This exercise will help you understand the concept of drawing a round form that has volume and solidity. If you are familiar with the concept, you can move on to drawing the pitcher. Using a similar set-up to the fish (Chapter 4), I looked at an orange and drew it.

You'll make a loose drawing of an orange that is lit from the upper right. Think of your orange as being solid and heavy. This will help you draw it with weight and mass.

Begin by starting a new 600 x 600 pixel file; then choose a medium gray (40–50% value) in the Colors palette.* In the Paper Selector (Toolbox), select Basic Paper,* and choose the Soft Pastel Pencil variant of Pastels. So that Painter can customize itself to the pressure and speed of your hand on the stylus and tablet, set up Brush Tracking.* Now sketch a rough outline of your orange. Keep your wrist loose.

2 **Adding the first tones.** Because it helps me to establish a balance or tension in my composition, I often prefer to rough in the darker shadow areas first, before modeling the overall subject.

Observe the light source shining from the upper right onto the orange. You'll use the same gray you chose for the sketch to suggest the deepest shadow areas on the side of the orange. Choose the Square X-Soft Pastel 20 variant of Pastels from the Brush Selector Bar, and using a light pressure on your stylus, lay in the shading for an even coverage on the side of the orange that is hidden from the light. Aim for a medium-gray value.*

LEARN MORE ABOUT. . .

* using the Colors palette. . . pages 46, 102
* using the Paper Selector. . . page 180
* Brush Tracking. . . page 52
* underpainting. . . pages 136, 162

The base tone, and layered darker values

The final highlights and shadows

Close-up detail of the final image

3 Layering values. Now rough in the foundation (underpainting) values by choosing a light gray and brushing it onto the lighter areas.* Then choose a darker gray and use gentle pressure on your stylus to paint curved strokes onto the shaded side of the orange.

4 Adding highlights and shadows. Continue to observe your subject, and model its surface using strokes that follow the rounded form. If needed, add darker values to the cast shadow in the area nearest to the orange. Brighten the "hottest" highlight with pure white. If you apply the white with a light touch on the stylus, you will

preserve the subtle tone and texture underneath. A cast shadow will help to place your orange on the surface. Paint your cast shadow darker nearer to the edge of the subject, and let it gradually fade out at its outer edge. Finally, remember that this exercise is a loose drawing, not a photo-realistic one. Relax and enjoy your drawing process.

Lighting and form. Setting up a single light source will make it easier for you to perceive the forms. You'll notice that the areas closest to the light are lighter, and that the object becomes darker in areas that are farther from the light. Directional lighting can make a huge difference in the appearance of a form. Here are four oranges in different positions, with a light source shining overhead. These sketches show that different dimensional effects can be achieved depending where the object is in relation to the light source. The brightest highlight will be the area closest to the light source. Notice the reflected light—light that reflects from the table surface onto the side of the object—and notice the darkest shadow on the object, which will be the area farthest from the light source, and directly under the subject.

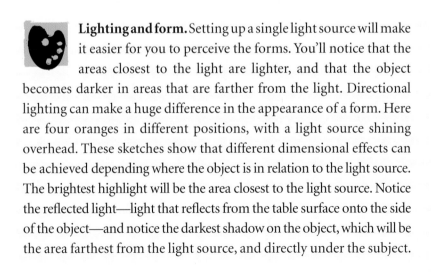

Drawing Rounded Forms

Pastel Medium Tip, small

*Pastel Medium Tip, default (top), **Pastel Medium Tip**, modified (bottom)*

Pastel on Charcoal Paper, default (top), Pastel on Charcoal Paper, modified (bottom)

ARTIST'S MATERIALS

Tablet: Medium pressure

Program: Photoshop

Paint: Grays chosen in the Colors palette

Brushes:

- Pastel Medium Tip: low opacity brush that applies subtly textured strokes

- Pastel Medium Tip: modified to cover underlying paint and to make stroke thickness vary with pressure

- Pastel on Charcoal Paper: low opacity brush with texture saved in the preset

- Pastel on Charcoal Paper: modified to cover underlying paint and to make stroke thickness vary with pressure

The first values

Building up darker values

1 **Setting up and laying in values.** Create a new file that measures 1500 x 2000 pixels. Choose a medium gray in the Color Picker, click on the Brush tool in the Toolbox, and choose the Pastel Medium Tip preset from the Dry Media Brushes. Set the Opacity to 100% in the Options Bar. Click to open the Brush Preset picker on the Options Bar, and reduce the size of the Pastel Medium Tip to about 5 pixels using the Master Size slider. Make a new layer, and draw a loose sketch.

Now click on the image background. Using the default Pastel Medium Tip preset, block in large areas of value, starting with the midtones. The midtones will help to unify your image, and will connect the lighter and darker values. I simplified the number of values at this stage, using a medium gray, a light gray, and a darker gray.

2 **Painting more values.** Before beginning to paint the darker values, I set the Pastel Medium Tip brush to vary its opacity with stylus pressure and saved the new preset.* While applying light pressure, gradually build up darker values, changing the size of the brush as you work. Let your strokes follow the curves of the forms.

Next, I feathered in the highlights on the side of the shaker and on its base. By applying very light pressure to the modified Pastel Medium Tip, I was able to subtly brush lighter value over the darker tones to give the impression of a blend.

LEARN MORE ABOUT. . .

* saving a brush preset. . . page 116

* pressure settings. . . pages 28, 65

Painting highlights and adding details

The final image

Close-up detail showing texture added

3 Painting the cast shadow and details. Next, to give the salt shaker more of a sense of space, I painted a gradation onto the cast shadow, and refined the reflected light on the edge of the base near this shadow and the underside of the shaker. Then I added more contrast to the edges of the shaker.

4 Adding texture and smudging. As a final step, I added a subtle texture to areas using the Pastel on Charcoal Paper preset. To brush more texture onto your image, choose the Pastel on Charcoal Paper preset. Open the Brush palette, and modify the brush so the Opacity varies with pressure.* Save your new preset. Now sample color from the

area where you want to paint and darken or lighten it slightly. You will achieve more texture if you apply a lighter pressure. Brush very lightly over the area to slightly blend tones and add texture. Photoshop does not allow you to smudge in the same way Painter does, but with carefully chosen colors, you can achieve a similar effect.

Painting with pressure. When using the Pastel Medium Tip, see what it's like to control the buildup of paint using pressure on the stylus. Choose the brush and click on Other Dynamics in the Brush Presets window. Then set the Opacity Jitter Control pop-up menu to Stylus Pressure. Experiment with the Opacity jitter slider if you like. (To slightly vary the opacity, I set it at 4%.) Save your new brush by choosing New Brush Preset from the pop-out menu and giving it a unique name.

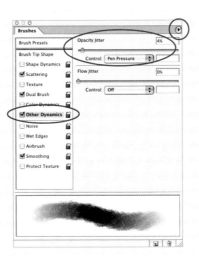

Drawing a Hollow Rounded Form

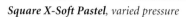

Sharp Pastel Pencil, *varied pressure*

Square X-Soft Pastel, *varied pressure*

Stroke smudged with **Soft Blender Stump**

A color digital photo of the pitcher with light source on the tabletop

A black-and-white version of the photo might help you to think in values instead of colors.

ARTIST'S MATERIALS

Tablet: Medium-soft pressure

Program: Painter

Paper: Sketchbook Paper: a versatile, medium-grain texture

Paint: Grays, chosen in the Colors palette

Brushes:
- Sharp Pastel Pencil: ideal for sketching; produces an expressive line that varies with pressure

- Square X-Soft Pastel: opacity and grain vary with pressure; the pastel strokes also change subtly, depending on the bearing (direction) of the stylus

- Soft Blender Stump: allows soft blending of values, while preserving subtle texture

1 Setting up a still life. In this exercise you'll use Pastel brushes to paint a three-dimensional pitcher that has volume and weight. Choose an object that has an obvious rounded form (such as a cup or a pitcher), and set it on a light-colored surface. I chose this vintage Bauer pitcher for my subject because of its rounded, retro shape and its interesting rings. I arranged the pitcher using a slight angle to add interest to the composition and to create intriguing negative space around it.

Position a small lamp that will cast an interesting shadow on the subject and table surface. I positioned the light source so it would shine from the upper left of the pitcher.

2 Visualize in black and white. Observe the lighting on your subject, and notice how the lighting enhances the presence of the forms in three-dimensional space. Study the tonal values of the blacks, grays, and whites and how they help to reveal the round body, rings, and hollow interior.*

LEARN MORE ABOUT...

* shading, tone, and value... pages 61, 64
* Brush Tracking... page 52
* using the Colors palette... pages 46, 102
* using the Mixer Pad... page 46
* using the Paper Selector... pages 32, 180
* cross-hatching... pages 77, 81–87, 105

The rough sketch showing basic shapes

The more refined sketch, showing the rings and cast shadow

3 **Sketching basic shapes.** Now create a new file with a white background. For a rectangular format like this one, set the Width and Height at 1400 x 1200 pixels.

After setting up Brush Tracking, I sketched the basic shapes of the pitcher using loose, simple strokes.* As you'll notice, I added an imaginary horizon line, which will help to create more of a sense of space.

Choose the Sharp Pastel Pencil 3 variant of Pastels, and choose the Sketchbook Paper from the Paper Selector (Toolbox).* Now choose a dark gray in the Colors palette, or mix it in the Mixer Pad.* Study your subject, allowing your eye to trace around its forms. (My pitcher was composed mostly of ovals and triangles.) Rough in the shapes and proportions to establish your composition. Keep your wrist loose, and apply more pressure to your stylus when you want to emphasize a line (by making it darker). Apply less pressure when you want lighter lines. As you draw, continue to take time to observe your subject and analyze its basic forms.

4 **Building a more detailed drawing.** When you have the proportions established, begin to refine your drawing. You can leave the lines you sketched earlier, because they will add character to your drawing. Drawing over the existing lines will also help you to refine your drawing.

As the drawing began to develop, I continued to use the Sharp Pastel Pencil, preferring to keep the strokes fine, so I could "sculpt" the forms. The rings function like "cross-contours," and help to add to the illusion of volume. If your pitcher does not have rings, you can still accomplish this by making your strokes follow the rounded forms—let them sweep curved lines around the pitcher. You could also accomplish this with cross-hatching, which would sculpt the form.* (Remember to carefully observe the perspective of the pitcher and to adjust the angle of the lines, as in the illustration above.) Continue to keep your wrist loose as you draw with your stylus so that you have a relaxed, natural feeling while sketching.

Painting broad strokes to lay in the first tones

Adding darker values to the shadow areas

5 Adding tone with pastel. Choose a Square X-Soft Pastel from the Brush Selector Bar. To give the still life atmosphere and space, use this pastel to paint broad strokes over the background using medium-value grays, (darker than most of the values in the pitcher). Darker values tend to recede, so they will help to bring the subject forward in the composition.*

To paint a stroke with a square edge, hold the stylus with its button up. To paint a stroke with a pointed end, hold the stylus with the button facing to the side (right or left). (To reduce the size of the X-Soft Pastel as you work, move the Size slider on the Property Bar to the left.) Continue to "sculpt" the forms by adding darker values.

I overlapped strokes using several directions to add activity and dappled light to the background. Next, I began to develop the forms of the pitcher using light to medium tones. I worked over broader areas first (for instance, the spout), and then gradually added more detailed strokes (the rings). Then I used similar grays to suggest a cast shadow.

Next, keeping my light source in mind, I began to add darker and lighter tones for more contrast. Study your subject. If your light source is positioned in the upper left like mine, consider adding lighter tones to the upper-left planes and darker tones to the lower-right planes.

Making a progress print. It's a good idea to make a print of your working image midway through your drawing process. At this point, I made an 8 x 10-inch print of my image because it's easy to become absorbed with reworking the details of a drawing on the computer, and to forget to zoom out and look at the entire image. After studying the still life and the print again, I decided to rework the bottom of the pitcher and to refine the cast shadow.

Redrawing the lower area of the pitcher and shadow

Brightening the highlight on the lip of the pitcher

6 Refining the pitcher, shadow, and background.
Using a dark gray and the Square X-Soft Pastel in a smaller size (12 pixels), I drew over the lower five rings of the pitcher to refine them. When I was satisfied with the look, I chose a light gray and added new highlights.

To blend areas of the pitcher and cast shadow, I switched to the Soft Blender Stump variant of Blenders. For subtle blending, apply a light pressure and work back and forth on the edge of the shadow to "feather" it, or make it more graduated. Pull out from the dark area into the light area using a heavier pressure when you want to pull some dark tone into a light area.

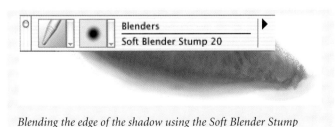

Blending the edge of the shadow using the Soft Blender Stump

When observing the pitcher, I noticed that the rim had some extremely bright highlights. To brighten these highlights in my painting, I used a small Square X-Soft Pastel and the Sharp Pastel Pencil. I zoomed into the spout area using the Magnifier tool, and carefully added very light gray and white pastel to areas of the lip and spout. (I chose not to go around the entire spout because it would not look natural.) Next, I added texture to highlights on the body of the pitcher. I chose the Square X-Soft Pastel 20, and lightly brushed a lighter gray over several of the rings of the pitcher. I also used the same pastel and varied light grays to add a gradation to the background behind the spout. Brushing very lightly (using a technique known as scumbling) allowed me to apply a little tone while revealing paper texture.* You can see the entire final image on page 58.

LEARN MORE ABOUT. . .

* shading and value. . . pages 61, 73
* Scumbling. . . page 104

White Orchid

6

SENSITIVE TONE AND MODELING

Making studies in black and white will help you to understand your subject and will lead to more successful work later when you use color. In this project, you'll set up a still life and practice the process of observing your subject and painting it with sensitive tone and modeling, giving it presence in realistic three-dimensional space.

 I drew White Orchid *using my favorite Wacom tablet and pen. The pressure-sensitive tablet used in combination with the Charcoal brushes in Painter allowed me to have control while drawing lines and building up interesting shading and texture on the flower petals. For the subject, I chose a beautiful white Phalaenopsis orchid and placed it near my computer. I lit the plant using a small lamp that I positioned on the upper right of the subject. Before beginning to draw, I studied the negative space around the orchid and its delicate forms that were enhanced by the lighting.*

My objective was to create a sensitive, expressive drawing, instead of a photo-realistic one. I chose to draw a single orchid, rather than the entire group that was on the stem, so that I could focus on one subject, and create a stronger statement. For a more dynamic composition, I exaggerated the angle of the orchid. Also, I exaggerated the value contrast to add drama and to enhance the focal point. I painted a cast shadow behind the flower using dark, multi-directional, hatched strokes, which added subtle interest, while increasing the depth.

Using Sensitive Tone and Blending

Hard Charcoal Pencil, varied pressure

Hard Charcoal Stick, varied pressure

Hard Charcoal Stick stroke blended using Soft Blender Stump, Pointed Stump, and Grainy Water

ARTIST'S MATERIALS

Tablet: Soft-to-medium pressure

Program: Painter

Paper: Basic Paper: a versatile, medium-grain texture

Paint: Grays, chosen in the Colors palette

Brushes:

• Hard Charcoal Pencil: ideal for sketching; opacity and texture vary with pressure

• Hard Charcoal Stick: allows subtle building of values, while revealing paper texture

• Soft Blender Stump: for blending larger areas

• Pointed Stump: for blending details

• Grainy Water: for blending while revealing paper grain

A color digital photo of the subject

A grayscale version of the photo might help you to think in black and white.

1 **Setting up a still life.** Choose a houseplant or a flower picked from your garden and set up your subject in front of a simple, non-distracting background. I chose this orchid as a subject because of its graceful shapes, unique texture, and interesting details. I found the shapes of the petals and the negative space around them to be fascinating.* I set up a small spotlight to cast interesting shadows on the flower.

LEARN MORE ABOUT. . .

* setting Paper Color. . . page 160
* the Colors palette. . . pages 34, 46, 102
* the Paper Selector. . . pages 32, 180
* Brush Tracking. . . page 52
* tone, value, and contrast. . . pages 73, 74
* textures to build value. . . page 77

2 **Visualizing in black and white.** Study your subject, allowing your eye to trace around the edges of the forms, and to take in the feel of the delicate texture. Absorb the affect of the lighting on your subject that enhances the feeling of its form in space. Study the tonal values of the blacks, grays, and whites and how they give the forms solidity.*

 Positive and negative spaces. Think of the forms of your subject as "positive space," and the area or "air" outside and around the subject as "negative" space. Positive and negative space are equally important to drawing and to good composition.

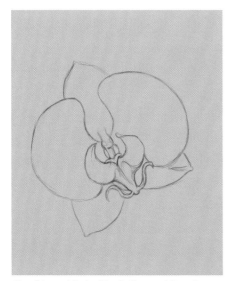

Sketching with the Hard Charcoal Pencil

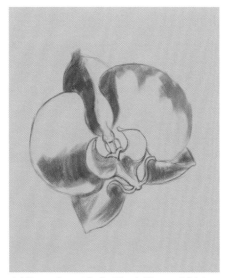

Adding value with the Hard Charcoal Stick

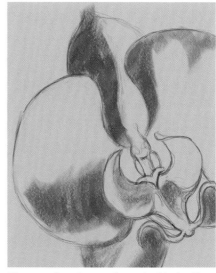

The curved strokes are shown in this detail.

3 **Sketching the shapes.** Open a new file that is 700 x 900 pixels. Set up a light-to-medium gray background color so that you can work with dark shadows and whiter highlights on a mid-toned ground.* Next, choose a dark gray in the Colors palette*, and choose Basic Paper in the Paper Selector.*

Set Brush Tracking to customize Painter to the feel of your hand on the stylus.* Then choose the Hard Charcoal Pencil variant of Charcoal from the Brush Selector Bar. Using your stylus, sketch in a way that is similar to how you would use a pencil, with lines that gently overlap one another to suggest the shapes. Focus on the simple shapes at this stage. If you like, embellish the most important areas by applying heavier pressure to create bolder strokes.

4 **Adding the first tones.** Now that the shapes are roughed in, you'll begin to build dimension by blocking in the first tones. For this task, I recommend using the Hard Charcoal Stick because of its rectangular, chisel-like shape, which allows you to expressively paint broad areas while revealing texture. You can build up value quickly or slowly, based on the pressure you apply to the stylus.

 For Photoshop users. If you don't have Painter, you can follow along with this exercise using Photoshop's Dry Media Brushes. Please see the sidebar on page 57 for how to load the brushes. I suggest using the Charcoal Pencil for sketching. Then try the Pastel Medium Tip preset for blocking in large areas of value. If you'd like to paint with more texture, try the Pastel on Charcoal Paper preset. (Although useful, the performance of the brushes will not be identical.) See the "Painting with pressure" tip on page 65 to learn how to set up this brush to vary opacity with pressure.

Sculpt the darkest areas of your subject first by using a dark gray. Observe and analyze your subject. Where are the darker values? (They are usually in the deepest shadow areas.)*

When painting the curved flower petals, I used curved strokes that followed the contours of the forms, as you can see in the close-up view above.

Developing more value

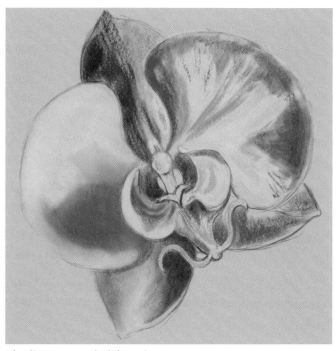

Blending tones on the left petal

5 Building form. Continue to observe your subject; study the values, from light to mid-tone to dark; and then carefully work the shaded areas to establish a value range. I added the mid-tone areas using the same gray color in the Colors palette, but used a lighter pressure on the stylus. If you prefer to build up the tone more slowly, lower the Opacity of the brush using the slider in the Property Bar. If your drawing still needs more contrast, darken the strongest shadowed areas.*

6 Blending. Use a Blender brush to subtly smudge or smear some of the areas, and blend the light and dark values. I suggest leaving traces of texture as you blend, by applying gentle pressure on the stylus. You will notice blended areas on the petals on the left of the flower in this example.

To blend with control in small areas, I suggest using the Pointed Stump; for blending larger areas, try the Soft Blender Stump or the Grainy Water variant of Blenders.

LEARN MORE ABOUT. . .

* blending. . . page 74
* the Colors palette. . . pages 34, 102
* textures to build value. . . page 77

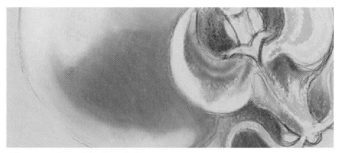

Close-up view of the blended area

Adding brighter highlights and deeper shadows

You can see the brighter highlights and deeper shadows in this detail.

7 **Adding highlight and shadow.** For a more dramatic, high-contrast look, I added stronger highlights using white and lighter gray tones.

Choose a bright white in the Colors palette and the Hard Charcoal Stick 10 variant of Charcoal from the Brush Selector Bar. (If needed, reduce the size of the Hard Charcoal Stick by moving the Size slider to the left in the Property Bar.) As you paint the brighter highlights, continue to use curved strokes that complement the forms. If you'd like to reveal more texture in some areas, as I did, apply less pressure to your stylus. To end a stroke showing more texture, gradually lift your stylus from the tablet at the end of the stroke.

After adding the highlights, you might want to add some deeper tones to the darker shadow areas if they need "punching up." In areas where you want a darker shadow without as much texture, reduce the size of the Hard Charcoal stick and apply more pressure. To achieve a crisper edge in some areas, I sampled color using the Eyedropper tool, and then zoomed in and used a small version of the Hard Charcoal Stick to carefully draw along the edges.

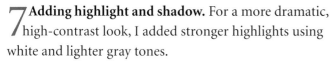 **Value, volume, and depth.** You can use value to suggest volume and depth. Darker values tend to recede, whereas lighter values will come forward. Strong value contrast will help to emphasize the focal point in a composition.

Painting the cast shadow and stem

Brightening details in the interior of the flower

8 Adding the stem and cast shadow. You may want to paint a cast shadow (as I did) to create more of a sense of space and atmosphere around the flower. For dappled light and interest, I used the Hard Charcoal Stick to paint varied angled strokes (wide, overlapping hatching marks) behind the left side of the subject.

Close-up view showing the angled hatched marks on the shadow

9 Emphasizing details. Again, it's a good idea to step back and look at your painting. Does your drawing need more contrast? Are there edges that you'd like to emphasize? At this point, I decided to emphasize a few important internal contours. I used the Hard Charcoal Pencil to strengthen edges of the highlighted interior curves, and I also redefined edges of the lower petals. The emphasized edge is most evident in the lower-left petal. Congratulations! You've completed the last step in this technique.

You've learned about using sensitive tone and value in your images. In the next chapter, you'll learn about creating the look of atmosphere in your images.

Using Interesting Strokes to Build Tonal Variations

There are many ways to build tonal variations, from blended gradations, to linear hatching, cross-hatching and stippling, to name a few. Here are some examples that can serve as inspiration for your own experimentation.

Layered hatching drawn with the Hard Charcoal Pencil: Linear hatching (top left), second layer of hatching applied (top right), third layer of hatching (bottom left), and fourth layer of hatching (bottom right)

Hatching drawn with the Hard Charcoal Stick 10: Overlapping linear hatching (top left), layer of light marks over dark (top right), soft angled hatching (bottom left), and angled lines, using harder pressure (bottom right)

Patched hatching drawn with the Hard Charcoal Pencil 5 builds tone and an abstract pattern

Overlapping tight circular squiggles drawn with the Hard Charcoal Pencil 5 build tone and suggest activity

Dots drawn with the Hard Charcoal Pencil 5 using varied pressure suggest a gradient with sparkle

Lines and dabs of different tones drawn with the Hard Charcoal Stick and Hard Charcoal Pencil using varied pressure add depth and interest

Expressive strokes drawn with the Hard Charcoal Stick 30 for tone and energy

Gradient drawn with the Hard Charcoal Stick 30 shows sketchy vertical strokes

Gradient (from left) blended with the Soft Blender Stump 20 (Blenders) for a softer look

Broad lines of darker tone drawn with the Hard Charcoal Stick 20 using varied pressure to create a subtle gradient

Conch Shell

7

A Sense of Atmosphere

You can achieve atmosphere in a variety of ways, two of which are cross-hatching (overlapping strokes that work together to build value) and pointillism (small dabs of tone that blend in the eye of the viewer). In this technique, you will simulate the effect of air, which is heavy with moisture or particles of pollen, and how it can add depth to an image. You'll use values of gray to draw with cross-hatched strokes, which overlap but do not cover the sparkling light and texture. This will give the drawing an amorphous, dreamy quality. For this project, you'll set up a still life and practice the process of observing your subject and drawing it so that it has shimmering light quality, as well as volume and mass. Following the feature project is a Painter sidebar, where you'll have the opportunity to put these concepts of light and texture to work.

I drew Conch Shell *from life using my favorite Wacom tablet and pen. The pressure-sensitive tablet used in combination with Chalk brush presets in Photoshop gave me control while drawing the shaded areas. For the subject, I chose a large, graceful conch shell, and placed it on a tabletop near my computer. Then I set up a small spotlight to shine on the shell.*

I use this approach when creating an atmospheric mood in a loose painting. As the drawing develops, the subject gradually emerges through layers of cross-hatched or dabbed strokes. Near the end of the process, I add a few linear details to bring areas into focus.

Building Atmosphere Using Hatching

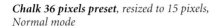

Chalk 36 pixels preset, *Normal mode*

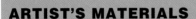

Chalk 36 pixels preset, *resized to 15 pixels, Normal mode*

A digital photo of the shell

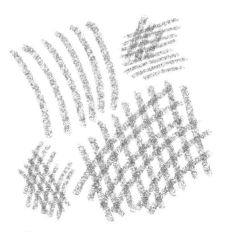

Chalk 36 preset strokes, Normal mode

ARTIST'S MATERIALS

Tablet: Medium pressure

Program: Photoshop

Paint: Grays, chosen from Swatches palette and Color Picker

Brushes:
- Chalk 36 pixels: ideal for pressure response; reveals Canvas texture saved with the brush
- Eraser: used to remove tone for highlight areas

1 Arranging a still life. Choose an object that has simple, intriguing forms (such as a sea shell or a pear with a unique shape), and set it on a light-colored surface. I chose this shell for my subject because of its graceful shape and its texture. Then I placed it at an angle to give the composition more depth, and to create interesting shapes in the negative space around it.

Position a small lamp that will cast a shadow on the subject and table surface. I positioned the light source to shine from the upper right.

 Which Chalk preset? Photoshop has several Chalk presets with similar names that perform very differently. For this exercise, use the Chalk 36 pixels preset.

2 Visualizing and setting up. Observe your subject. Notice how the lighting helps you to observe the forms in three-dimensional space.

Now start a new file with a white background. For a square format like mine, set the Width and Height at 1500 x 1500 pixels, and set the Mode menu to Grayscale.

Next, choose the Brush tool in the Toolbox, and then open the Brushes palette (Window > Brushes). Click on Brush Presets, and scroll to find the Chalk 36 pixels preset. This brush has a canvas texture saved

LEARN MORE ABOUT. . .

- using the Brushes palette. . . page 26, 116
- stroke variations. . . page 77
- choosing a color. . . page 26

Chalk 36 preset strokes, Dissolve mode

Medium-tone hatching, without darker shading or details

with it, which allows you to draw textured strokes, similar to hard charcoal on canvas board. Choose a dark gray in the Swatches palette (Window > Swatches). (I chose 65% gray.) In the Options Bar, change Mode to Dissolve. Using your stylus, practice making hatching strokes. Experiment with lowering the opacity if you like. (I varied the opacity from 40–80% depending on the density of tone I wanted to paint.)

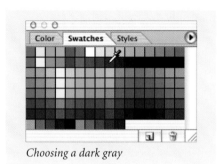

Choosing a dark gray

3 **Building a sense of atmosphere.** This atmospheric approach uses both line and mass to build a composition. Overlapping hatched lines blend in the viewer's eye to create areas of tone that sparkle with light.

Using a light touch on your stylus, use cross-hatch strokes to lay in the background first. The shape of the object should begin to emerge. Starting with the background, or the negative space around the shell, will help you to see the shape of the shell apart from the background as you sketch. Continue to observe your subject and analyze its basic forms. This method will keep your drawing loose. Don't focus on detail in this stage; continue to work overall your drawing, until your basic composition begins to emerge. I added a few

very loose strokes to suggest the contours of the shell. I planned to draw over the light strokes later with darker tones.

 Texture with Dissolve. The default painting mode is Normal. For this drawing, I changed the mode to Dissolve using the pop-up menu in the Options Bar because it allowed me to retain a crisper texture while building up the layers of hatching.

Drawing light-medium tones using hatching strokes

Close-up of the light-medium toned strokes

4 **Modeling form and space with hatching.** For more dimension, add darker hatched strokes to the background, and begin to add more value to your subject.

I overlapped strokes, using several directions, to add activity and dappled light to the background. Because darker values tend to recede, this helped to bring a lighter subject forward in the composition.*

Resizing a brush. To resize your brush as you work, click to open the Brush Preset Picker in the Options Bar and then use the Master Diameter slider to adjust the size. (I used the 36 pixel size for broader areas, and then reduced the size to 20 pixels for modeling areas of the shell, and then to 15 pixels for more detailed areas.) You can also use the Bracket keys on your keyboard to resize a brush. To reduce the brush size, press the left bracket ([), and to increase the size, press the right bracket (]).

Now that the composition was established, I began to sculpt the forms of the shell. I recommend using broad cross-hatching strokes to sketch the larger areas of the subject first (for instance, in my image, the curves above the opening of the shell). Then gradually add thinner hatched strokes (I added curved hatched strokes on the opening of the shell, and the thinner lines on the top protrusions).

When drawing your subject, "sculpt" the forms by building up curved hatching that follows the direction of the forms.* If you've chosen to use lighter values on your subject, as I did, consider leaving pure white areas for the highlights.

LEARN MORE ABOUT. . .

* value and depth . . . page 75
* modeling form. . . pages 64–65

Using hatching strokes to build up medium tones and basic forms

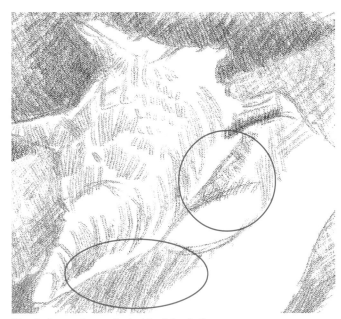

The darker strokes on the inside of the shell

Next, to build more dimension, I added darker tones to the background, cast shadow, and the shell in a few places. For this task, I chose a darker gray swatch (75% gray) in the Swatches palette. As you work, layer the strokes, but be careful not to fill in areas with solid gray. You will add darker gray to a few areas in the last step.

Keeping my light source in mind, I used overlapping linear strokes and cross-hatch strokes to darken the opening edge of the shell. I paid careful attention to the curved forms and to the raised and indented areas as I worked.

 Rescuing an overworked area. If you've overworked an area of your drawing, it's easy to step back a few stages using the History palette. (If the palette is not open, choose Window > History.) Click backward in the history states until you have undone the overworked strokes. (The default number of history states is 20. You can increase this number in Preferences, but Photoshop requires more memory with a larger number of states.) You can also switch to a small Eraser

Stepping back in the History palette

and use the same cross-hatching stroke pattern to "hatch" the light areas back in.

Adding darker tones to the background, the cast shadow, and the shell

Modeling more detailed forms on the shell, and darkening the opening

5 Refining the shell and background. Consider making a print of your image when the forms and background are established. After making a print of my image and studying the shape of the shell, its proportions, and values, I noticed that the upper "horn" of the shell needed to be redrawn and more highlights needed to be brought out in some areas. I set up the Eraser tool in Brush mode with a 9 pixel hard-edged tip; then I saved a preset for the Eraser tool.* Using this Eraser (in sizes of 9–15 pixels), I sketched hatching strokes to sculpt the highlights.*

 The Eraser tool and the Wacom stylus eraser. If you turn your pen upside down and use the eraser on your stylus, Photoshop will choose the default Eraser tip or the most recent Eraser tip that you've used. To set up my Eraser for this project, I chose the Eraser tool in the Toolbox, and then chose the Hard Round 9 pixel brush tip in the Brush Preset window. I could easily switch between my Brush tool and the Eraser by turning my stylus as I worked.

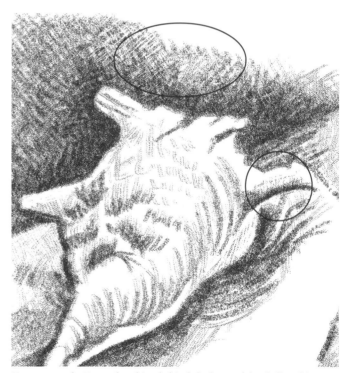

You can see the Eraser hatching behind the horn of the shell and in a few places on the body of the shell.

The top horn of the shell needed to be corrected

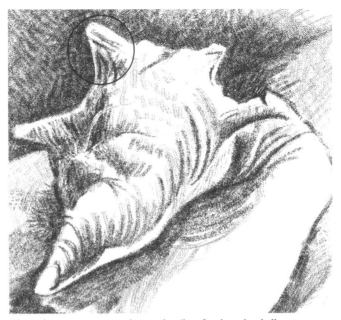

The redrawn top area, and more details refined on the shell

6 **Redrawing areas and adding more contrast.** If you notice areas of your image that need to be redrawn, continue to observe your subject as you make the refinements. After any corrections are complete, add the final details. For editing flexibility, you might want to draw these final details on a new layer, as I did.*

After removing tone from the horn area, I used a 15 pixel version of the Chalk preset and sketched with 75% gray to redraw the horn, and I added detail to the raised areas below the horn. Next, I used a smaller brush and a darker gray to refine a few details on the interior of the shell, and I also embellished the curved shapes leading into the opening of the shell. As a final touch, I strengthened a few edges, including the edge of the cast shadow and the left side of the shell.

LEARN MORE ABOUT. . .

* Eraser tool presets. . . page 31
* Eraser tool modes. . . page 94
* layers. . . page 26

A close-up view of the redrawn horn, and the raised and indented areas on the outside of the shell

Achieving Sparkling Light

Square Soft Pastel 30, soft to firm pressure

Square Soft Pastel 10, hatching

A digital photo of the apples

Using hatching to start the basic composition

1 Setting up and visualizing. Choose an object that has a rounded form (such as an apple or a orange), and set the object on a light-colored surface. Position a lamp that will cast a shadow on the subject and table surface.

Now, create a new file with a white background. For a rectangular format like this one, set the Width and Height at 1800 x 1400 pixels. From the Brush Selector Bar, choose the Square Soft Pastel variant of Pastels, and choose Charcoal Paper from the Paper Selector.

 More atmosphere and light. This Painter technique is a variation on the atmospheric concept described on pages 80–81. Painter allows more complex layering of pastel or chalk-like media (without covering texture) than Photoshop does, so it's an ideal tool to use for this atmospheric approach.

Then, using the Colors palette and Mixer palette, I created a palette of grays.*

 Mixing grays. You can create grays for your value studies using the Mixer. (To open the Mixer, choose Window > Show Mixer.) Choose grays from the Color Wells at the top of the palette or from the Colors palette. Apply them to the Mixer Pad using your stylus and the Brush tool in the Mixer palette. Use the Palette Knife tool to blend your gray paints.

A palette of grays

LEARN MORE ABOUT. . .

* using the Mixer. . . page 46
* Brush Tracking. . . page 52

Working more values in the background, and onto the apples

Roughing in the cast shadow and adding more tone to the apples

2 **Laying in general forms and space.** After setting up Brush Tracking, use cross-hatch strokes to lay in the basic composition, roughing in a graduated background and the general light on your subject.* Try to keep your strokes loose, using the cross-hatch method and avoiding adding details at this early stage. Adjust the brush size as needed using the Size slider in the Property Bar.

3 **Building space and form.** Next you'll use darker grays (about 80%) and more cross-hatched strokes, because they will weave a pattern of sparkling light and create a wonderful sense of space. If you use a light touch on the stylus, you won't completely cover the texture or values underneath. Use curved strokes that follow the forms when painting the apples.

Building layers of modeling on the apples and values on the background

Adding subtle detail to the apples

4 **Modeling with smaller hatched strokes.** To deepen the values on the apples, I used a darker gray, and applied it using shorter strokes, focusing on the deepest shadow areas on the apples, and also the darkest areas of the cast shadows. Next, I used a lighter gray to emphasize the gradient on the right side of the background.

5 **Finessing and adding details.** Your finished image should not look photo-realistic, but it should have an amorphous quality with a feeling of shimmering light. As a final touch, I used a variety of grays and a smaller brush size to add details (such as the stem), and to strengthen a few edges.

The Port du Val Cliffs and Beach at Etretat

8

STARTING WITH A SCANNED DRAWING

In the first part of this chapter, you'll learn how to scan a drawing that you can use as a basis for artwork in the computer. In the first technique, you'll rework a scanned drawing in Photoshop to resolve its composition, and then use the reworked sketch as the starting point for a loose, boldly colored study completed in Photoshop, reminiscent of the traditional technique of combining opaque watercolor (or gouache) and transparent watercolor with a drawing. For the second project, you'll start with another drawing and paint right over it using the Oil Pastel brushes in Painter and develop a painting with energetic brushwork and atmosphere. Following these two projects are helpful sidebars that demonstrate how to paint watercolor washes over a drawing.

 For many years, I had dreamed of visiting the small town of Etretat on France's Normandy coast. Etretat, with its spectacular limestone cliffs, was a favorite painting location of many of my favorite master artists—Eugene Delacroix, Gustave Courbet, and Claude Monet, among others.

In 2000, my husband and I visited this scene at Etretat several times. I loved the towering limestone cliffs, the negative spaces around the arch and needle, and the way the light-colored cliffs picked up the light at different times of the day. I sat on the beach and drew on Vellum finish Bristol board and in my sketchbook using HB and 2B graphite pencils. The Bristol and sketchbook have subtle texture and are ideal surfaces for drawing with pencils. To record details and different moods, I drew several sketches. The drawings have now become the basis for a series of color paintings of the area. After scanning the drawings, I used a Wacom tablet and pen, and Painter and Photoshop to color the drawings and to create the paintings.

Scanning a Pencil Drawing

The raw scan of the close-up sketch of Etretat

The scanning process digitizes an analog image by sampling data into pixels, making it available for use in Photoshop and Painter.

How will your scan be used? Before beginning to scan, you should know how you will use the scan, and if you plan to incorporate it into another image, how large that final image will be. (Please refer to the sidebar on pixels and resolution on pages 7 and 8.)

The Epson 4870 scanner I used has a handy software plug-in that allows scanning directly into Photoshop. (Many other manufacturers have plug-ins, as well. There are many different scanner interfaces, so you might need to do some experimenting.) I chose File > Import > SilverFast Epson SE. My drawing measured 6 X 4 inches.

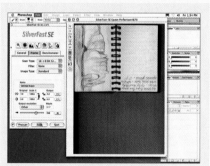

The SilverFast software for the Epson 4870 scanner set up to scan the 4 X 6-inch pencil drawing at full size and at 500 ppi

Because of its small size, I set the resolution at 500 pixels per inch—which would capture the detail that I wanted into a 3000 X 2000-pixel file. From the Scan Type pop-up menu, I chose the 16>8 bit grayscale mode, which would capture the subtle range of grays in the drawing. The spiral-bound sketchbook

with loose pages was challenging to get the sketch perfectly straight on the scanner. No worries! We can easily straighten a scan in Photoshop.

Straightening and cropping. To automatically adjust the straightness of your scan, choose the Measure tool (it's nested with the Eyedropper tool) and drag out a measure line along the top of the scan, and then choose Image > Rotate Canvas > Arbitrary. Photoshop will enter the correct angle of rotation into the Rotate Canvas dialog box. To crop your scan, choose the Crop tool. Set the tool to its defaults by clicking the Clear button. Now drag a marquee around the area that you want to keep, and then double-click inside the marquee (or press the Return or Enter key) to accept the crop.

The scan of the sketch with editing complete

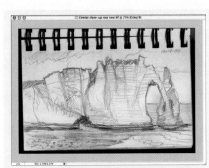

The crooked, raw scan (above) and the straightened, cropped scan (below)

LEARN MORE ABOUT. . .

* pixels and resolution. . . page 8
* color modes. . . pages 95, 101

Adjusting the tonal range. For more contrast, I reduced the gray tones in the sketch (while preserving the texture of the pencil marks) using Photoshop's Levels command. Choose Image > Adjustments > Levels. If the white paper in your drawing looks muddy, choose the White Point Dropper and click a blank paper area. (It's also possible to set the white point in the scanner software if you choose.)

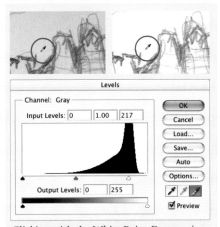

Clicking with the White Point Dropper in a light area of the drawing brought it back to white, and changed the Input Level (originally 255) to 217.

Adding Canvas Size. I wanted to add more image to the sky and water, so I chose Image > Canvas Size, and increased the Height and Width of the scan.

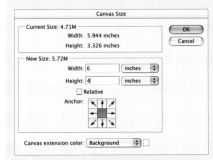

Increasing the Canvas Size on the top and bottom of the image

Using Photoshop to Work Over a Pencil Drawing

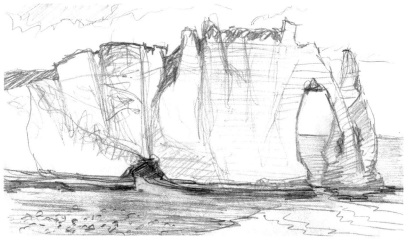

The scan of the close-up sketch of Etretat

Spatter, *58 pixels, Normal mode, used in various sizes and opacities*

Tapered Spatter, *58 pixels, Normal mode, used in various sizes and opacities*

My scanned drawing had a lot of texture, which would work well with the painting that I planned to do in Photoshop.

I planned to integrate the sketch into the image by making it semi-transparent and coloring it with a sepia tone that would complement the color theme. Leaving the pencil texture in the sketch would add interesting texture and tonal values to the image, which would help the color have more personality.

After I painted areas of flat color for an underpainting, I planned to overlay semitransparent glazes that would model form and create depth.

1 **Drawing and scanning.** In the previous spread, I told the story of how I drew the sketches while traveling in France. Likewise, you can choose a sketch from your sketchbook, or use pencils and paper to create a new drawing to scan.

I drew the pencil sketch shown above in my 4 x 6-inch travel sketchbook. After scanning the drawing into Photoshop at 500 pixels per inch at actual size, in grayscale mode,* I cropped the scan and adjusted its tonal range.*

LEARN MORE ABOUT. . .

* scanning. . . page 90
* cropping an image. . . page 90
* adjusting tonal range. . . page 91

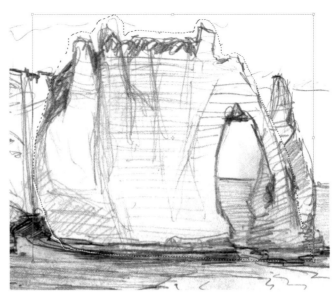

Using the stylus to draw the freehand Lasso selection

Using Free Transform to give the towers more height

2 **Transforming for a more dramatic perspective.**
Take time to examine your image. Would you like to refine the composition of your drawing? Will your composition have more impact if you change the size of one of the elements?

For more drama in my drawing, and to enhance its focal point, I increased the height of the towering cliffs at the end of the point.

To transform an element, choose the Lasso tool and use your stylus to draw a freehand selection around the area that you want to edit. The stylus is extremely useful for drawing selections because it gives you much finer control and is faster to use than a mouse.

Next, choose Edit > Free Transform, and while pressing the Shift key (to constrain the proportions), use the Move tool to change the size. (I increased the size of the "towers" by pulling on the handles.) When you have adjusted the Free Transform handles as you like them, double-click inside the marquee (or press the Return or Enter key) to accept the transform. Now deselect the

selection by choosing Ctrl/Cmd-D. After the transform—in preparation for the painting to come—I cut the final drawing to a layer, leaving the Background white.* (The instructional sidebar below describes how to cut the sketch to a layer, and how to copy it to a layer. For this technique, it's best to cut it to a layer.)

 Putting your drawing on a layer. You'll have more flexibility during the painting process if you put your drawing on a layer. To cut the final drawing to a layer, leaving the Background layer white, choose Select > All, and from the Layer menu, choose New, and then Layer Via Cut (Shift-Ctrl/Cmd-J). To copy the drawing to a layer and leave a copy on the background, choose Select > All, and from the Layer menu choose New, and then Layer Via Copy (Ctrl/Cmd-J). To rename your new layer, double-click on the layer name, and when the text field appears, type a useful name into the field. (I named my layer "sketch.")

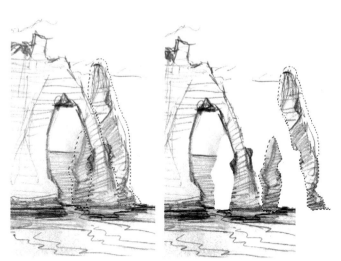

Selecting the needle, (left), and the needle moved (right)

The needle is moved outside the arch and redrawn.

3 Selecting and moving the needle. You can improve your composition by moving elements in your image. (To create interesting negative shapes around the arch and the needle, I moved the needle outside the arch.) Using the Lasso tool and your stylus, draw a freehand selection around the area you want to move, use the Move tool to drag it (I moved the needle to the right), and then deselect.

 Cleaning up. To clean up areas of the drawing (for instance, the sea waves, the needle, and the beach), I used the Eraser tool with a hard-edged tip, in various sizes.

Notice the areas between the wiggly water lines in the illustration above, and the fine scratch marks near the base of the needle.

4 Redrawing the needle and other elements. Now that your elements are where you want them, you can use the Brush and Eraser tools to redraw areas of your image. With the Brush tool chosen in the Toolbox, click the brush "footprint" in the Options Bar to open the Brush Preset picker, and choose the Hard Round 9 pixels preset. Press Alt/Option to switch from the Brush to the Eyedropper, and sample a dark gray color from the image.

Using a dark gray color sampled from the image and a small Hard Round brush, I sketched in the missing areas on the needle, and strengthened the lines on the edges of the arch. Next, I used the Hard Round preset to draw a few more sketchy gray lines and to embellish the shadows at the base of the cliffs. I chose the Eraser tool in the Toolbox, and then I selected the Hard Round 9 pixels tip, and cleaned up a few areas using the small Eraser. Then I used a tinier 5-pixel Eraser to scratch into the base of the needle and cliff to emphasize the stratification.

The reworked drawing, ready for color

The drawing colored with sepia

5 Coloring the sketch with sepia. Coloring your drawing helps integrate it into your painting. I planned to use a color theme that included warm browns, so I gave my sketch a sepia brown color, which worked well with the color palette I planned to use.

Before coloring the sketch with sepia, change the Color Mode to RGB, and preserve the layer.* (Because it was easier to complete the edits on the gray file, I didn't add the sepia before cleaning up and editing the scan.)

Tint your drawing by filling the "sketch" layer with sepia.* Then set the blend mode of the "sketch" layer to Multiply in the Layers palette so the white areas of the sketch appear to be clear, allowing you to use your sketch as a guide when you paint color on underlying layers later.

LEARN MORE ABOUT. . .

★ Color Modes. . . page 95, 101

★ blend modes. . . page 27

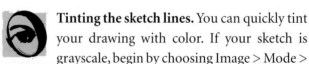

Tinting the sketch lines. You can quickly tint your drawing with color. If your sketch is grayscale, begin by choosing Image > Mode > RGB. (Don't flatten the image when changing the Mode.) In the Layers palette, target the sketch layer; then in the Color Picker, choose a warm, dark brown for the Foreground Color (I used R 70, G 58, B 51), and choose Edit > Fill, with Foreground Color; Mode, Color; and Opacity, 100%. The Color Mode fills your sketch with transparent color while preserving the tones in your drawing.

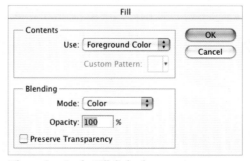

The settings in the Fill dialog box

The paint dabs in the upper-left corner of the image

The warm orange-ochre base color is laid in on the new layer.

6 Designing a color palette. Think about the kind of color palette that you'd like to use. Will it feature warm browns and oranges like mine, or will it include cooler blues and purples? I remembered how the afternoon light lit up the white cliffs with a golden glow. I would need a rich, earthy color palette to carry out this color theme.

I recommend adding a new layer to store your paint dabs, as you plan your color theme. Use the Color Picker to mix colors; then make small dabs of paint in an upper corner of the image. (If you choose to leave the paint dabs on this layer, you can hide or show the layer as needed when you want to sample color from it using the Eyedropper. You can also save your colors into a custom Swatches palette and then delete the layer.

LEARN MORE ABOUT. . .

* using the Color Picker. . . page 42
* adding a new layer. . . page 26
* saturation. . . page 42
* value and depth. . . pages 75, 82
* Brushes palette. . . pages 27, 116
* saving a preset. . . page 116

7 Laying in an opaque base color. In this step, you'll paint a base color (underpainting) that will establish the color theme for the entire image. (I used a warm orange-ochre color.) Choose the Brush tool, and then choose the Spatter 59 pixels preset and scale it up to about 85 pixels. Make a new layer and name it "base color." Using loose, broad strokes, block in color behind the sketch. (When you complete a stroke and lift up on the stylus, you'll notice the bristle marks at the end of each stroke.)

Next, make a new layer for the sky, and name it to keep your painting organized. Choose a medium sky

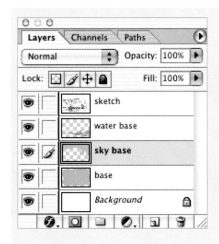

I used three layers for the underpainting: the base, the sky base, and the water base. I set all of the underpainting layers to Normal blending mode. The sketch layer sits on top of the layer stack, and I set its blending mode to Multiply.

The sky is roughed in on another new layer.

Adding the first shadows to the cliffs

blue from your color palette. (I chose a blue that would be dark enough to contrast with the cliffs.) Using the same brush as before, block in the sky. Scale the brush smaller to work in the tighter areas at the top of the cliffs and inside the arch. (I scaled my brush down to about 25 pixels.) Now add a new layer for the "water base." For the water, I chose a cool, blue-green hue from my palette about the same value and saturation as the sky.* I envisioned the water moving as I painted it. I left the broken areas of the waves alone for this stage, so that when I painted them with lighter color later, some of the underpainting would show through.

The underpainting for the water is laid in on its own new layer.

8 **Adding darker tones and shadows.** Now add a new layer and begin to paint darker tones for the shadows. As you paint, vary the size and opacity of the brush as needed. On a new layer, I painted darker tones on the water, cliffs, and beach. I wanted to paint energetic strokes of varied thickness to define the crevices on the cliff and the moving water, so I made a tapered version of the Spatter preset.* To vary colors, I sampled from each base color and made the color a bit darker and more saturated using the Color Picker.

 Making a tapered brush. To make a Spatter brush that paints thick and thin strokes based on pressure, open the Brushes palette and choose the Spatter 59 pixels preset. Click on Shape Dynamics, and then enable the check box. Now set the Size Jitter Control pop-up menu to Pen Pressure. Save your new preset by choosing New Brush Preset from the palette menu. I named my brush "Tapered Spatter."

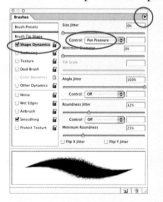

Painting the first tints of lighter ochre on the cliffs

Adding more glazes to the light areas on the cliff face

9 **Adding semitransparent tints and highlights.** Now you'll use tints and glazes (and a technique similar to conventional watercolor) to build dimension in your painting. Add another new layer and name it "glazes." Choose the Tapered Spatter brush, and reduce its opacity to about 20% in the Options Bar. Sample color from your image, and then use the Color Picker to make it lighter or darker. Using varied pressure on your stylus, paint expressive brushstrokes. Let your brushstrokes be fun, squiggly, and energetic. This is a loose, expressive study, not a tight rendering.

I remembered the mass of the towering limestone cliffs. For more interest on the cliff face, I added lighter tones and highlights using the glazing technique. After mixing a lighter version of the ochre, using the Color Picker, I used the low-opacity Tapered Spatter preset in various sizes to brush and dab color onto the cliff face. I used shorter, dabbed strokes to suggest the indentations in the cliff and rocks on the beach. To emphasize the horizontal striations on the cliff, I varied the pressure on my stylus while painting a few graceful strokes of varied thickness. Making areas of the cliffs lighter would help bring them forward in the composition, and would also enhance the focal point.

You can see the varied ochre tints and lighter highlights on the cliff face and on the needle in this detail.

I painted these graceful strokes with the Tapered Spatter brush using 100% opacity (top) and reduced opacities (bottom).

Adding darker purple and turquoise to the base of the cliff

The complete final image with the darker blue and purples added

10 **Adding more glazes and details.** What does your image need? Do you want to add darker shadows, or more foreground detail? To create more depth, consider adding darker tones behind your subject (as I did behind the "cliff towers.") Using the Spatter preset in various sizes, I brushed thin glazes of darker color onto the sky. For most of the glazing, use a low-opacity (12%) version of the brush. Making the clouds darker behind the lighter cliffs helps to enhance the focal point. Use a smaller version of the brush and varied opacity to refine details.

To finish the painting, I painted curved brushstrokes of darker turquoise on the shaded areas of the waves. Then I sampled rust color from the cliff area, and used thin, curved strokes to suggest the reflection of the cliff on the water, while keeping in mind the motion of the waves. The completed final image is shown in the upper right.

Step back and take a good look at your painting. Congratulations! You've completed the technique.

Paint blending and layers. For the look of blended paint, I used several layers in Photoshop. With Painter, you need fewer layers because you can blend and make the media interact more easily.

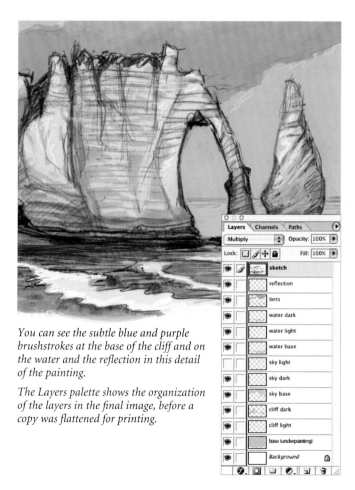

You can see the subtle blue and purple brushstrokes at the base of the cliff and on the water and the reflection in this detail of the painting.

The Layers palette shows the organization of the layers in the final image, before a copy was flattened for printing.

Using Painter to Work Over a Pencil Drawing

Chunky Oil Pastel, *30 pixels, using various sizes and opacities*

Variable Oil Pastel, *30 pixels, using various sizes and opacities*

This scanned drawing of the Port du Val at Etretat has a broader view of the beach.

This technique was inspired by my traditional experience with conventional pastel and oil pastel. Here I've combined a scanned pencil drawing with digital oil pastels in Painter. I colored the scan with a dark sepia brown that blended with the color theme. After painting with the oil pastels, I composited the sketch with the image because it would contribute value and detail.

LEARN MORE ABOUT. . .

* scanning. . . pages 90–91
* cropping an image. . . page 90
* adjusting tonal range. . . page 91
* using the Mixer. . . page 46

1 Drawing and scanning. Draw a detailed sketch. (I drew the pencil sketch shown above on 9 x 12-inch vellum-finish bristol board.) Now scan your drawing into Photoshop. My settings were 300 pixels per inch, at actual size.* Then crop your scan and adjust its tonal range.*

Copying your sketch to a new layer. To put a copy of your sketch onto a layer for safekeeping, choose Select > All, hold down the Alt/Option key, and choose Select > Float. To rename your new layer, double-click the layer's name in the Layers palette, and enter a new name in the Layer Attributes dialog box.

The sketch colored with the Sepia Browns gradation

Adjusting the tones. You can use the Equalize feature in Painter to adjust the tonal range of your scan. To add more contrast to your sketch and reduce gray tones, choose Effects > Tonal Control > Equalize. When the Equalize dialog box appears, move the black point marker and the white point marker under the histogram closer together to reduce the gray tones. Move them right or left to affect the line thickness and quality. You can preview the adjustment in your image before you click OK to accept.

2 **Coloring and making a layer.** For this study, tint the sketch with a color that will complement the color palette you plan to use in your painting (I chose a warm sepia brown).*

Next, put a copy of the sketch onto a layer, leaving the original on the Canvas.* Reduce the Opacity of the layer to 20% using the Opacity slider on the Layers palette; and then

Automatic color mode conversion. Painter's native color mode is RGB. If you open a grayscale scan in Painter, the image will be converted automatically to RGB color.

temporarily turn its visibility off in the Layers palette, so you can see the pastel strokes more clearly as you begin to paint over the drawing.

Coloring with sepia. Open your scanned sketch in Painter. Click the Gradient Selector near the bottom of the Toolbox, and choose the Sepia Browns gradient from the list. With the selector still open, open the palette menu to the upper right of the gradient list, and choose Express in Image from the menu. Then click OK. The Sepia gradient will automatically be mapped to your image.

Using the Colors palette and Mixer (left), and trying out colors with the Chunky Oil Pastel over Basic Paper texture (right)

Blocking in the first light tones

3 **Mixing paint and trying out colors.** You can use the Mixer palette* to try out colors on-the-fly as you paint. The Mixer features an oily brush to apply color and a palette knife to blend paint.

In this technique, you'll use the texture-sensitive Oil Pastels that can blend and smear color, so it's a good idea to experiment with how these Oil Pastels will react with the texture on an image as you try out the colors. Open a new file (mine was 700 X 1000 pixels) and try out the Chunky Oil Pastel and Variable Oil Pastel variants of Oil Pastels using your stylus. Experiment with color until you settle on a color theme that you like, and your "palette" is complete. For this painting with soft, warm light, I chose a color theme of primarily pastel colors; a few brighter, more saturated colors; and a few grays and browns.

LEARN MORE ABOUT. . .

* using the Mixer. . . page 46

4 **Laying in paint over the sketch.** To begin painting, choose the Chunky Oil Pastel variant of Oil Pastels and block in color right over the top of the original sketch on the Canvas. (If I painted over an area completely and then needed to see it, I could always make the sketch layer visible, and turn up its opacity.) I recommend using light- and medium-toned colors with lower saturation for the underpainting. This will create a rich layering of color as you build up more Oil Pastel strokes over the underpainting.

A sense of atmosphere. In this project, you will use an atmospheric technique that employs hatched strokes to build the volume of the land mass and to suggest the planes of rock. The layered brushwork will also create shimmering light on the beach and water. For variations on this technique, see Chapter 7, "A Sense of Atmosphere."

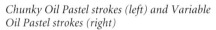

Chunky Oil Pastel strokes (left) and Variable Oil Pastel strokes (right)

Beginning to model the forms of the cliffs

5 Understanding the brushes. The Oil Pastels offer great expressiveness when combined with a tablet. Vary the pressure on the stylus, and these brushes vary the opacity and also reveal more or less grain. The Chunky Oil Pastel slightly smears new color into existing paint, and it has an uneven broken edge, just like a traditional, crumbled soft oil pastel. The Variable Oil Pastel allows a natural-feeling stroke that changes as you rotate your hand while painting, and it allows you to smear new color into existing paint more easily. Experiment with the brushes by making squiggly lines, while varying pressure. Notice how wonderfully the colors blend as you overlay the colored strokes.

6 Sculpting the forms. Look at your sketch, and plan how you'll sculpt the forms. The Variable Oil Pastel 30 has a rectangular tip that makes it ideal for blocking in the crevices and cracks near the top of the towering cliffs. Using the Variable Oil Pastel 30, paint the larger crevices. Begin at the top and pull a stroke down, while slightly rotating your wrist as you paint. You'll notice a wonderful variation in the density of the stroke. When you've painted the deeper, darker top crevices, switch to a smaller brush—the Variable Oil Pastel 20. To suggest the horizontal stratification on the cliff face, use lighter pressure.

Looking at my sketch and remembering the crevices and indentations in the cliff face, I began modeling the cliff by pulling medium-toned purple strokes vertically down the top crevices. The cliff also had intricate horizontal stratification, which I chose to simplify, by painting subtle horizontal strokes in just a few areas.

Painting vertical brushstrokes while rotating the stylus and varying the pressure

Defining the arch and needle

Adding brighter color to the horizon, and darker shadows to the arch and needle

7 **Adding brighter color and deeper tones.** Next, use both brushes as you add more color. Switch back and forth between the Chunky Oil Pastel 30 and the Variable Oil Pastel 30, as you continue to block in the planes on the cliffs. I added warmer colors to create an afternoon glow on the cliffs, and on the backlit arch in my painting.

Smearing and scumbling with Oil Pastels. When you apply a new color, the Variable Oil Pastel can smear the new color into the existing paint, which is helpful when building up layers of varied color. The pressure you apply affects smearing. If you apply heavy pressure, more new color is applied. If you use medium pressure and pull at the edge's existing color, you smear more color. The Chunky Oil Pastel smears more subtly. Both of these Oil Pastels paint a grainier stroke when you apply a light pressure, which is useful for scumbling new color over the top of existing pastel.

Blocking in a large shaded area on the cliff using a purple-gray

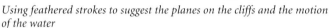

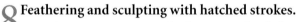

Using feathered strokes to suggest the planes on the cliffs and the motion of the water

Painting overlapping feathered strokes of blues, greens, and purples in light and mid-tone values on the water

8 **Feathering and sculpting with hatched strokes.** Now that your painting is laid out, step back from the image to look at its overall composition. Do you need to add more detail or contrast in certain areas? Is there movement in the brushwork to help guide the viewer's eye around the composition?

To add movement and varied color while sculpting the forms of the cliffs, I overlaid cross-hatched strokes, using a conventional pastel technique known as feathering. I wanted to create motion in the water, rather than have it appear smooth. The water was moving up and down on the beach, so I lightly sketched in light aqua and blue horizontal strokes, varying the brush work using slight angles. I used the Variable Oil Pastel, and sized the brush smaller to lay feathered strokes over the top. By varying the pressure on my stylus, I was able to control the opacity of the brushstrokes. (This brushwork is shown in the illustration on the right.)

Painting the beach and water using feathered hatched strokes of varied colors, creating shimmering light and color on the beach and in the water

You can see the reflected light and the final linear details on the cliffs in this close-up view.

Using similar colors on the sunlit areas of the cliff and the beach helps to carry the effect of the soft afternoon light, as shown in this detail

9 **Adding final details.** It's good to make a proof print before completing your painting, so you can see where you want to paint final accents and details. My proof print showed me where to add darker tones; for instance, in the small cave, the lower crevices, and at the base of the arch.

Before beginning to paint your final details, add a new layer, and position it above the Canvas and below the sketch layer. Then, using a small Variable Oil Pastel, paint the details that your image needs.

I darkened the cave, the crevice, and also added definition to the outer edge of the arch. Using more saturated purples and oranges and golds, I used the Variable Oil Pastel 20 to add lively accents of varied color to the beach and water. The water was moving up and back, rising and falling on the gently curved beach. To emphasize the motion of the surges, I added short overlapping angled strokes. These layered strokes added more complexity, giving the water a more natural, shimmering look with broken color. This brush-work is shown in the upper-right illustration.

The angled, hatched strokes overlap, and are drawn using many directions. This helps to suggest the layers of limestone rock on the cliff. Layers of overlapping strokes also help to build the reflection. It is sketched right over the top of the moving water.

The grainy, scumbled texture on the sky lends to the atmospheric effect. Hatched strokes help to sculpt the rounded hills, and angled strokes add energy and character to the planes on the shady cliff face.

The overlapping strokes of purples, grays, and golds add interest and color activity to the beach. Thick and thin horizontal and angled strokes add motion to the waves, and squiggly lines suggest the rolling surf line.

Next, I used varied pressure to paint thin strokes of light orange and gold (using the Variable Oil Pastel 10) on the cliff face in areas where it was hit by the sun, and in areas where light reflected on the cliffs from the water. I also added loose overlapping angled strokes to the gently curved beach. Then I used a small Variable Oil Pastel to add gentle, curved strokes to suggest the rolling surf line, where the waves spilled onto the sand.

To carry the reflected light to the foreground, I recommend using similar colors to those you used to paint the brighter accents on the cliffs. Finally, add more texture to the sky by "scumbling" with very light blue pastel. Here's how: Choose the Chunky Oil Pastel, and a color that is different from the underlying color. Apply light pressure to your stylus as you paint new color just on the peaks of the paper texture, over the top of the existing color.

You can see the entire final image on page 88. In the next four pages, you'll learn about painting washes over a drawing. Then you can take a break, or move on to the next chapter.

The final image. To achieve a look of oil pastels with a complex texture, I needed only a few layers. The sketch layer contributes subtle line work to the composition, and sits at the top of the layer stack in the Layers palette, with its opacity set to 20%.

Adding Washes to a Drawing Using Painter

The Port du Val viewed from the west

Painter's Digital Watercolor is ideal for painting light tints over scanned drawings, such as this pen-and-ink sketch. I laid in light-colored washes over the ink drawing quickly and was able to blend paint easily and smoothly.

1 Setting up. Open a scanned drawing, and cut the drawing to a layer by choosing Select > All and then Select > Float. Set the layer Composite Method to Multiply in the Layers palette. Then click on the Canvas in the Layers palette.

I recommend that you use color tints with a value of 50 or lighter when working with Digital Watercolor. This sky blue has a value of 80.

For most of the coloring, it's a good idea to use light tints that will set off the ink drawing. Choose a light blue for the sky; then select the Digital Watercolor category in the Brush Selector Bar. For the washes, choose the Soft Broad Brush variant.

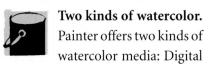 **Two kinds of watercolor.** Painter offers two kinds of watercolor media: Digital Watercolor and Watercolor. Digital Watercolor is faster and simpler to use. It can be painted on the image Canvas or on a default layer set to Gel mode. Watercolor requires its own special media layer and allows for more realistic watercolor effects like media pooling and runny, dripping pigment, which are amazing to watch and to paint with!

Digital Watercolor brushstrokes

Watercolor brushstrokes

Laying the first washes and brushstrokes on the Canvas

2 **Painting washes.** Using light-to-medium pressure on your stylus, paint soft strokes on the sky and water using the Soft Broad Brush. You can vary the opacity of the paint with the pressure you apply to the stylus.

Using the Soft Round Blender to smoothly blend the water

3 **Blending and smoothing.** Choose the Soft Round Blender and use a light pressure on the stylus to pull and smooth paint. I pulled my strokes using various directions to emphasize the lighting on the water.

The washes on the Canvas are complete.

4 **Adding more washes.** Using the Soft Broad Brush, continue to lay in washes over all your painting. If you want crisper-edged strokes, try the Simple Water variant. For a diffused effect, try the Soft Diffused Brush.

The darker washes painted on a new layer

5 **Painting glazes.** Add a new layer (in Gel mode) and use the Simple Water and Soft Broad Brush to apply a few darker glazes. (I applied glazes around the edges of the image, leaving the center lighter to enhance the focal point.)

Applying Washes to a Drawing Using Photoshop

The Port du Val viewed from the west

Color Picker

Select foreground color:

Choosing a light blue in the Color Picker

In this exercise you'll use transparent washes on layers to create a watercolor look over a drawing.

Glazing on layers. I painted glazes on several layers, each set to Multiply to allow the colors to blend. Photoshop does not allow the same interaction with media (smearing, blending, or diffusing) that Painter has, so glazing on layers is a great solution to achieve paint interaction. Using layers also helps with editing flexibility.

The Layers palette for the final image

1 Getting set up. Open a scanned drawing, convert it to RGB color mode, and cut the drawing to a layer by choosing Select > All and then pressing Shift-Ctrl/Cmd-J. Set the layer Blending Mode to Multiply in the Layers palette. Then make an empty new layer to hold the first washes, and set it to Multiply.

Just as you might with conventional watercolor, I recommend starting out with light color tints and then

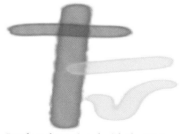

Flatter brushes. These default brushes allow you to paint thick and thin strokes depending on how you rotate the stylus, which makes them nice for calligraphic brushwork, such as the motion lines on the waves.

Watercolor Loaded Wet Flat Tip strokes

gradually building up to darker-toned washes as the painting develops. Choose a light blue for the sky, and then select the Watercolor Small Round Tip from the Brush presets. To paint the broader wash areas, I sized this brush up to 72 pixels, and saved the larger-size preset so it would be easy to choose later. I also saved a 40-pixel version of this preset. For the first washes, choose the 72-pixel preset.

Brushstrokes painted with the Watercolor Small Round Tip, sized to 72 pixels. This default brush is named "round" but it is actually elliptical.

Using a large round preset to paint the first washes on a new layer

2 **Painting broad washes.** Using medium pressure on your stylus, paint light tints on the sky and water using the Watercolor Round 72 preset. I used light colors and reduced paint opacities, from 10–40%.

The underpainting layers are complete in this step.

3 **Completing the underpainting.** After adding a new layer (in Multiply mode), use the Watercolor Round in sizes from 20 to 72 pixels, and medium pressure on your stylus to lay in the underpainting for the cliffs and the hills.

Painting details on the cliffs and beach using a smaller brush

4 **Painting darker glazes.** After adding new layers (in Multiply mode) for the cliff glazes, the hills, and the beach, use a smaller Watercolor Round to paint darker glazes on the landforms.

Adding slightly darker washes to the water on a new layer

5 **Adding final glazes.** Now add a new layer for the final shadows. Use the Watercolor Round and Watercolor Loaded Wet Flat Tip brushes to apply a few darker glazes. (I added shadows to the beach and activity to the water.)

The Three Engines

9

USING A PHOTO REFERENCE FOR PAINTING

In this project, you'll use a photo reference as a guide for sketching and painting. You'll set up a still life and photograph it, and then create a palette of colors and build custom brushes to use with a tablet and stylus. After that you'll use the photo as a guide for sketching and painting. To organize the illustration, you'll separate the elements of the image—the photo, sketch, loose color, and details—on individual layers, so that you can make changes to one without affecting the others. Following this project, there is a Painter sidebar that demonstrates using the Tracing Paper feature as a guide while sketching and painting.

 I painted The Three Engines *in Photoshop using custom brushes and my favorite Wacom tablet and pen. The pressure-sensitive tablet used in combination with the custom-built brushes and Photoshop's paint engine allowed a great deal of control and expression in creating a wide variety of brushstrokes.*

I developed this colorful, expressive approach especially for product illustrations of children's toys and clothing. The technique involves analyzing the objects and reducing them to simple shapes in a sketch, and then painting the shapes using areas of flat, loose color. For this illustration, I used my nephew Brady's train engines on a light-colored surface. I lit the engines using a full-spectrum light shining from above and to the right of the engines. Carefully observing the light and how it subtly changed the colors on the shapes helped me develop the dimension of the forms.

My approach to the illustration was interpretive rather than photo-realistic, with lots of experimentation with color and brushwork. I used a palette of primary colors (red, yellow, and blue), with some pastels and secondary colors as accents. The primary and pastel color palette added to the playful feeling of the illustration.

CP

Using a Photo Reference While Painting

Sketcher, *varied pressure*

Gouache, *varied pressure*

The original digital photo

ARTIST'S MATERIALS

Tablet: Medium-soft pressure

Program: Photoshop

Brushes:

- Sketcher: made from Photoshop's Hard Round 5 customized with pressure response and texture for loose, expressive line work

- Gouache: made from Photoshop's Soft Round 100 customized with a sampled dab and pressure response for applying flat, opaque coloring to simulate gouache or oils

- Gouache: modified for painting fine, textured details

- Gouache: modified for applying transparent color

1 **Setting up and photographing a still life.** Start out by setting up a still life on a light-colored surface. A full-spectrum light casts interesting shadows on the surface, which is a technique often used for product shots. (If you don't already have one, you can buy a full-spectrum light from a home improvement store.) After you've set up the still life, either photograph it with a digital camera, or use a camera with film and then have the photos saved on a CD-ROM as part of the film processing.*

Open your photo in Photoshop. If you like, you can crop it or change its dimensions.*

To set up a digital "lightbox" for sketching, first make sure the background color is set to white. (Press the "D" key.) Then move the photo to a new layer by pressing Ctrl/Cmd-A to select all, and then Shift-Ctrl/Cmd-J to cut the image to a new layer, leaving behind a white background. (If you do not see a white background, set the background color to white in Transparency and Gamut Preferences.) Reduce the new layer's Opacity to 40% in the Layers palette.

To help keep track of your layers as you build the file, it's a good idea to give each layer a meaningful name. Double-click on your new layer's name in the Layers palette and type Original Photo.

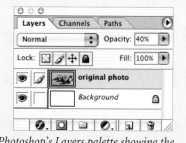

Photoshop's Layers palette showing the "lightbox" setup

LEARN MORE ABOUT...

* the file size you need. . . pages 8–9
* cropping in Photoshop. . . page 90
* resizing in Photoshop. . . page 9

Experimental dabs of paint color

Marks made with the pressure-sensitive brushes

2 **Choosing colors and making a "palette" file.** To begin experimenting with color, create a new document with a white background.* Choose the Brush tool from the Toolbox, and then click on the Foreground color swatch at the bottom of the Toolbox to open the Color Picker.* Choose colors from the Picker, or sample them from the Original Photo layer (with its Opacity restored to 100% in the Layers palette)* and make pigment dabs in your new file.

Try out colors until you settle on a color theme that you like, and your "palette" is complete. Then save the file. When you paint (in steps 5 and 6), you can sample color from your palette file, or you can make a custom Swatches palette.*

Reducing the colors by posterizing. It can be difficult to accurately sample color in a photo. For instance, you might click with the stylus in what looks like a uniformly red area, but the sampled color may turn out to be darker or lighter than expected. To make it easier to sample, add a Posterize Adjustment layer to reduce the number of colors: Click the Create New Fill or Adjustment Layer button at the bottom of the Layers palette. Try out different settings (between 4 and 8 Levels) until you get a set of colors that you like. At any time, you can click in the eye column of the Posterize layer to turn its visibility off or on. Or double-click on the layer's thumbnail* and change the number of colors. Use the Dropper tool to sample colors from the photo layer.

3 **Making brushes.** Before you start painting, you'll need to build two brushes specially designed to take advantage of a pressure-sensitive tablet and stylus. You'll need one brush for loose sketching and one for applying flat, opaque color like that of gouache or oils. Both brushes will increase in size as you apply more pressure, so you can easily make your brushstrokes thick, thin or tapered. "Making Brushes for Sketching and Painting" on pages 116–117 explains how to build these brushes.

Continued on page 118

LEARN MORE ABOUT. . .

* using the Color Picker. . . page 42
* using the Swatches palette. . . page 26
* using the Layers palette. . . page 26

Making Brushes for Sketching and Painting

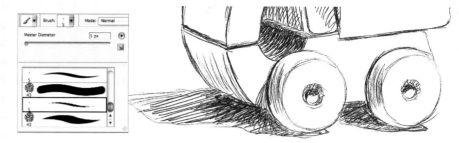

Strokes made with the sketcher brush

To start building brushes, first choose the Brush tool from the Toolbox. Then open the Brushes palette (Window > Brushes).

A brush for sketching. To make a brush that's good for loose sketches, you'll make it responsive to stylus pressure and you'll build in texture to make it look like your pencil is interacting with the surface of the paper.

The sketching brush is based on Photoshop's Hard Round 5 pixels brush, so click on the Hard Round 5 pixels preset in the Brushes palette.

The Brushes palette with the Brush presets displayed, shown using Small List view

To set the controls so that the brush-stroke gets wider as you apply pressure to the stylus, click on the name Shape Dynamics (not the check box, but the name) in the Brushes palette, and in the Size Jitter Control pop-up menu near the top of the panel, choose Pen Pressure.

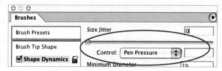

The Brushes palette Shape Dynamics panel showing the control for size set to Pen Pressure

To build in some paper texture, click on the name Texture in the Brushes palette. Choose the Wrinkles texture, which performs much like a traditional drawing paper when it is scaled down.

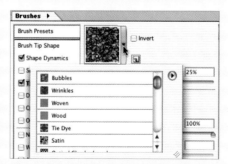

Choosing the Wrinkles texture. The texture list is shown using Small List view.

Wrinkles is a fairly coarse texture, but you can get a finer-textured look by reducing it to 25% using the Scale slider. Leave other settings at their defaults.

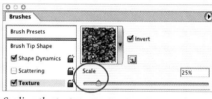

Scaling the texture

There's one more thing you have to do to make sure your new brush is available in the Brushes palette and the Brush Preset picker so that you can choose it whenever you want to draw with it: Click the little arrow to the right of the Brushes palette name and choose New Brush Preset from the palette's menu.

Adding your brush to the Brushes palette

In the Brush Name dialog box, name your brush (you could call it Sketcher), and click OK.

Strokes made with the gouache brush

Sketcher and gouache used together

A gouache brush with a custom, "captured" brush tip. This pressure-sensitive brush applies flat color with subtle bristle marks. Instead of starting with one of Photoshop's existing brushes, you'll start this brush by creating a round custom "bristly" tip in a new file. Open a new document (Ctrl/Cmd-N) with Height and Width set at 72 pixels and Resolution set at 72 pixels/inch.

Make a round selection with the Elliptical Marquee tool. (To constrain your selection to a circle, press the Shift key.) Make sure to leave several pixels of space between the edge of the selection and the edges of the file. Choose the Brush tool (press "B"), and then choose the Soft Round 100 pixels brush from the Options Bar's pop-out Brush Preset picker. In the Options Bar, change the Mode to Dissolve and the Opacity to about 75%.

Modifying the Soft Round 100 pixels brush to make a "bristly" dab. The Options Bar shows the Preset picker and the Mode and Opacity settings.

Now click inside the round selection in the file you created.

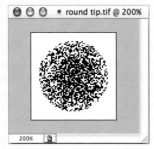

Painting a custom tip inside the circular selection boundary

Next, using the Rectangular Marquee tool, make a selection around your brush tip image. Choose Edit > Define Brush Preset, and give your new brush a name (such as Gouache). The size of the sampled dab determines the size of the new brush.

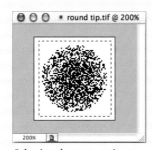

Selecting the custom tip

Brushes with sampled tips usually must have their Spacing adjusted to paint smooth strokes. You can do this in the Brushes palette by clicking on the name Brush Tip Shape and

reducing the Spacing to between 6–10%. Additionally, open Shape Dynamics, and in the Size Jitter Control pop-up menu near the top of the panel, choose Pen Pressure.

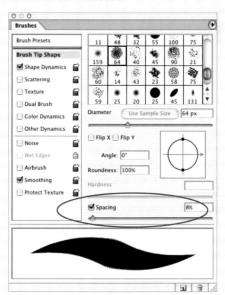

The Spacing adjusted in the Brush Tip Shape section

Add your new gouache brush to the Brushes palette and Brush Preset picker, just as you did for the sketcher. You'll notice two gouache brushes in the Brush Preset list. Click on the first one with the looser spacing in the presets list, and choose Delete from the Brush palette menu.

Sketching using the "lightbox"

The completed sketch, with visibility for the "original photo" layer turned off

4 Sketching. Next, you'll sketch the basic forms of your subject. You can then use your sketch as a guide for painting, instead of constantly looking at your photo.

With the Brush tool chosen in the Toolbox, click the brush "footprint" in the Options Bar to open the Brush Preset picker, and choose the sketcher brush that you made in step 3. Use the Color Picker* to choose a dark gray color for sketching.

Better observation. If you can, leave your still life set up as you paint. Observing your subject from life and toggling the visibility of the reference layer on and off while painting gives you a different perspective on your subject, helping you to become better acquainted with its forms and color nuances.

Make an empty, new layer for your sketch (Ctrl/Cmd-Shift-N), and rename it Sketch by double-clicking its name in the Layers palette. If your new sketch layer isn't at the top of the Layers palette, drag its name up to that position.

The Layers palette with the Sketch layer added

Now draw a loose sketch. Let your hand move in a relaxed and expressive manner as you draw with the stylus. Press lightly to draw a lighter, thinner line, and heavier to sketch a thicker, stronger line. The reduced

opacity of the Original Photo layer (set up in step 1) makes it easy to see your contrasting dark gray sketch lines. You can toggle the Original Photo layer on and off by clicking in its eye in the Layers palette.

Visibility turned off for the Original photo layer and Posterize 1 layer

LEARN MORE ABOUT. . .

* programming your stylus. . . page 28–29
* changing brush size. . . page 82

Beginning to lay in flat color areas

The first flat color areas roughed-in

The roughed-in color, including shadows

5 Roughing-in the color. Now add another empty layer, this time for painting, and drag this new layer under the Sketch layer in the Layers palette. Name it Loose Color to help keep your Layers palette organized, as you did with the other layers in steps 2 and 3. If you like, you can merge your Posterize Adjustment layer with your photo layer (as I did), by selecting it in the Layers palette menu and choosing Merge

The Layers palette showing the Loose Color layer added and visibility of the Original Photo layer turned off

Down. Now you can click the eye icon to hide your Original Photo layer.

To lay in areas of flat color, choose the Brush tool (press "B"). Then click on the brush footprint in the Options Bar, and select your gouache brush preset from the Brush Preset picker. To make the pigment look opaque like gouache, make sure the Opacity of the brush is still set to 100% in the Options Bar and Mode is set to Normal.

Load your brush with paint by holding down the Option/Alt key and clicking in your "palette" file (from step 2) to sample color; then release the key and paint. Or use the rocker button on your stylus, programmed to act like the Option/Alt key.* As you paint, you can also sample existing color from your painting, instead of just your "palette" file.

Your brushstroke will change as you vary the stylus pressure. But to work with a larger or smaller brush, you can change the overall size range of the brush by opening the Brush Preset picker on the Options Bar and adjusting the Master Diameter slider, or by using the bracket keys to increase or decrease its size.*

As you observe your subject or your reference photo, look carefully at the shadows. You will see subtle reflected light, rather than solid gray. In areas of the multicolored shadows where you want more complexity, you can make the pigment partially transparent by moving the Opacity slider in the Options Bar.

Adjusting size and opacity of the gouache brush

The in-progress loose color for Engine #1 with the sketch turned off

The color for Engine #1, showing the reworked shadows and background

6 Completing the loose color. At this point, you can turn off visibility for the Sketch Layer (unless you decide to keep the sketch lines as part of the illustration).

I continued to refine the painting. For instance, I added brighter color overall in the image. Then, using a steadier hand on my stylus, I cleaned up a few edges on the trains. I was careful not to overwork the clean-up process, because I did not want the painting to look mechanical, but to have a hand-painted look. I subtly reworked the shapes in the shadows to be more simple, pleasing curves that would complement the composition. Also, I toned down the shapes and colors in the background by using a low-opacity version of the gouache brush to paint a wash of warm gray behind the trains, which helped to enhance the focal point. Then I added a few linear details using a smaller version of the gouache brush.

 A consistent texture. For a realistic, consistent look overall, plan to use the same texture at the same scale for any textured brushes that you use to paint a particular piece. That way, all brushes will seem to "reveal" the same paper texture.

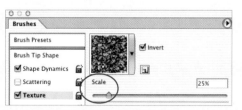

The "Wrinkles" texture, scaled to 25%

The completed painting for Engine #1 with textured details

A detail of Engine #2 showing the textured brushwork

7 **Adding more details and texture.** Next, add another new layer to your file, and name it Details. Drag this layer above the Loose Color layer. By painting details on a separate layer, you can experiment with finer brushwork without changing the Loose Color layer below. Choose the Brush tool and the Gouache brush preset. Reduce the brush size using the Master Diameter slider in the Brush Preset picker, as described in step 5. To add a subtle texture to the strokes of this smaller gouache brush, open the Brushes palette (Window > Brushes) and click on the word Texture. Then click on the texture thumbnail and choose Wrinkles; finally, scale it to about 25%. Save this new brush preset as "Gouache with texture."

Where does your painting need details? Where would adding texture complement your image? Using your stylus, press harder where you want a thicker line and gradually decrease the pressure when you want to taper a line. I used this approach when painting the brighter highlights on the wheels.

For most of the linear details, I used a small, smooth Gouache brush (without the texture), saving the textured brushwork just for accents. In the final image, I used a medium-sized, smooth Gouache brush to add richer darks in the shadows under the

The final Layers palette showing the Details layer selected

Close-ups of the completed painting for Engine #2 and Engine #3, including the linear details and textured brushwork. The texture can be seen on the blue trains, on the edges of the highlights, and more subtly on the front of the yellow train.

trains. I also painted brighter highlights along some of the edges where the light was the strongest. To paint shiny highlights on the metal screws on the wheels, I used almost pure white. Finally, I sampled color from the image and added textured edges to some of the flat color areas, such as the light green areas of color on the two engines. I also added a few textured details to the highlight areas on the red and yellow engine, as I finished the painting.

You've done it! Step 7 is the last step in this technique. I hope you've enjoyed the painting process. In the sidebar on the facing page, you'll see how easy it is to simulate the look of gouache in Painter. You'll be able to apply the painting processes you've learned in this chapter in the later projects in the book.

The long journey of the "digital lightbox." Many artists who use the computer and a tablet and stylus also use digital or scanned photos, incorporated into their painting files as a reference while sketching. Although the digital technology is quite recent, this "tracing" technique goes back a long way. Master painters have used various forms of cameras and photography as references for their paintings, ever since those technologies became available. Vermeer, for instance, used the camera obscura. More recently, master painters developed the technique of projecting a photo onto a canvas, to help them map out a composition. And illustrators have long used light tables and luci-graphs to trace proportions from photo references. Using a photo on a layer in a digital file is just the latest step in a long journey.

Using Painter's "Digital Lightbox"

The Tracing Paper feature in Painter was designed to help you trace a reference image quickly. It's also useful when painting with Painter's cloning brushes.*

The reference photo

The cloned image with Tracing Paper enabled, and the in-progress drawing

The final illustration painted with the Gouache brushes. The sketch layer is hidden.

1 Setting up for tracing. For this exercise, begin by opening a reference photo. Make a clone by choosing File > Clone, and leave your original image open. (Painter's powerful cloning function includes an important feature, called Tracing Paper.) To sketch as I did, delete the contents of the clone Canvas by choosing Select > All and then pressing Backspace/ Delete. Enable Tracing Paper by choosing Canvas > Tracing Paper or pressing Ctrl/Cmd-T. Next, make a new transparent layer for your sketch by clicking the New Layer button at the bottom of the Layers palette.*

2 Sketching and painting. Now choose a dark gray in the Colors palette, and the 2B Pencil variant of Pencils in the Brush Selector Bar. Using your stylus, draw a loose sketch.

I added a new layer and painted colored brushwork using the Gouache brushes. If you like, use the Dropper to sample colors from your photo. First, I laid in the large, flat areas of color on the body of the engine using the Flat Opaque Gouache 20 brush. To paint the smaller areas, I used the Fine Round Gouache

LEARN MORE ABOUT. . .

* cloning. . . pages 179, 183
* making a new layer. . . page 34

10 brush, varying its size as I worked. Toggle Tracing Paper off and on as you work so that you can see the color in your painting more accurately. (The Tracing Paper toggle button is in the top right of the image window.) The Gouache brushes offer a variety of expressive strokes when used with a tablet and stylus.

A close-up detail of the blue train illustration

Sunrise

10

DEFINING THE FOCAL POINT

These projects demonstrate the thought process behind the composition design of two paintings that have strong focal points. You'll begin each painting using your own reference sketches. In the first project, you'll use Photoshop to paint an image that has a limited color palette, and then you'll create a sunlight effect on a layer and composite it using a transparent layer mode to enhance the focal point. For the next project, you'll create a blended pastel painting in Painter, and learn creative painting and composition techniques such as underpainting, color modulation, and lighting effects.

 I painted Sunrise *in Photoshop using custom brushes and my favorite Wacom tablet and pen. The painting was inspired by the courageous fishermen who take their boats out through the challenging surf in Baja California.*

In addition to referring to reference sketches for inspiration, I remembered carefully observing the light at the time of day and how it subtly revealed the forms. I chose a limited palette of colors that helped to establish a dramatic feeling in the painting. For Along Tomales Bay, I was inspired by the beautiful design of waterways in the marshes near Tomales Bay in northern California. For a calm, restful feeling, I used a cooler color theme of mostly blues and greens, and I used Painter's Pastels and Blenders brushes to paint smooth, soft color transitions.

My approach to both paintings was interpretive rather than photo-realistic. To achieve the painted effects, I did a lot of experimentation with both color and brushwork. In both paintings, I used traditional composition techniques, and designed both compositions to lead the viewer's eye into the paintings.

Strengthening the Focal Point in a Photoshop Painting

The inspirational colored pencil sketch

***Sketcher**, Normal mode, used in various sizes and opacities*

***Gouache**, Normal mode at 100% (left), and Multiply mode at 25% opacity (right)*

ARTIST'S MATERIALS

Tablet: Medium-soft pressure

Program: Photoshop

Brushes:
- Sketcher: customized with pressure response and texture for loose, expressive line work

- Gouache: customized with a sampled dab and pressure response

- Gouache: modified for applying transparent color

- Eraser: used to scratch and "feather" highlight areas

For *Sunrise*, I designed a composition with the focal point off center, with beams of sunlight shining down, focused on the central boat. To invite the viewer's eye into the composition, I painted the light area on the lower right, with the light area moving up through to the central boat and deeper into the composition. To create tension and a more dramatic composition, I built the inverted "v" shape of the light from above shining on the fishermen in the boats. Also, I used atmospheric perspective (less contrast, detail, and color saturation in the distant hills) to give more attention to the boats that had more detail and contrast.

1 **Assembling references and designing the composition.** To begin, draw conventional sketches and scan them, or if you prefer, draw directly in Photoshop using the "Sketcher" brush you made in Chapter 9.*

If you've scanned a drawing, cut the image to a layer* so you can lower the opacity of the reference and use it as a guide while tracing and reworking the composition.

If you choose to sketch directly in Photoshop, open a new file and add a new transparent layer for your sketch. Drawing on the layer gives you more flexibility with how you incorporate your sketch into the image.

The colored pencil sketch I used as a loose reference for the beach

The digital sketch shows the reworked cliffs, boats, and foreground.

I drew the colored pencil studies shown above on location in my 8 x 10-inch travel sketchbook. The blue and yellow sketch notes the inspiration for the color theme and the composition, including the sun rays, which help to define the focal point. The brown sketch notes more detail on the hills and cliffs. After scanning the blue drawing into Photoshop at 300 pixels per inch at actual size, I cropped the scan.* I used the brown drawing for reference but did not bring it into my image as a layer.

I liked my references, but I wanted to change the cliffs, boats, and foreground, and combine some of the elements from both sketches. To design the composition,

I added a new layer and drew a black-and-white sketch using the "Sketcher" brush. As you see in the digital sketch above, I have opened up the right foreground area and have moved the boats down in the image. I used the second sketch as a reference while loosely sketching the forms of the cliffs and hills.

For Painter users. If you don't have Photoshop, you can follow along with this project using the Fine Point variant of Pens to draw the digital sketch. For the color painting, try using the Gouache brushes, reducing their opacity when needed to achieve the semitransparent washes. For truly transparent washes, try the Digital Watercolor brushes. You can paint the transparent washes on a new layer, with its composite method set to Gel. (The performance of the brushes will not be identical.)

LEARN MORE ABOUT. . .

* scanning. . . pages 90–91
* Sketcher brush. . . pages 114, 116
* Gouache brush. . . pages 114, 117

You can see the golden base color in this image.

This image shows the shadow color painted on the distant hills.

2 **Adding a base color to the study.** The yellow-gold base color is the underlying color for my image; it sets the mood for this painting with golden light. To give your image a base color, add a new layer and position it directly under your sketch layer. (I named my layer "gold base.") You can use the Gouache brush* that you made in Chapter 9 (or the Oil Medium Wet Flow default preset, scaled to a larger size) and rough color in by hand using your stylus, or you can fill the layer with color by choosing Edit > Fill.

3 **Laying in the shadows.** To achieve atmospheric perspective where the far away hills recede into the distance, use less contrast than you will use in the foreground and focal point areas. Because the painting depicts sunrise with a lot of dark areas (except the area illuminated by the sun), there will not be many high-contrast details in the darker shadow areas. (I painted the details in the shadows using subtle changes in value.) For this time of day, I recommend using a limited color palette. Choose a dark purple or brown that will work well with the gold base. (I chose purple because it would mix with the golden colors and create a variety of browns, when color was added using a low-opacity brush.)

LEARN MORE ABOUT. . .

* atmosphere. . . pages 78–87
* Gouache brush. . . page 117

Blocking in the shadow areas on the painting

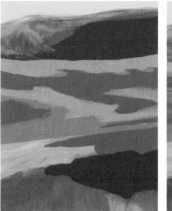
Painting glazes on the hills using brushes in Multiply and Normal modes

Add a new layer and position it directly above the gold base layer in the Layers palette. (I named my layer "purples.") Using the Gouache brush in Normal mode and in various sizes, paint brushstrokes to block in the darkest shadow areas, progressing from the back of your composition (farther away) to the mid-ground and foreground.

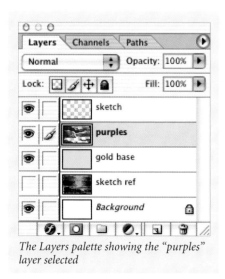
The Layers palette showing the "purples" layer selected

4 **Adding subtle detail to the hills.** To paint transparent color on the darker areas of the hills, use a small Gouache brush in Multiply mode, at a low opacity from 10–30%. To paint light color over dark, use the Gouache brush in Normal mode, at a low opacity from 10–30%. The low opacity allows you to build up color slowly, as I did, and to apply the color in glazes, much like traditional watercolor. I varied the colors, using both warm (red-purple), cool (blue-purple), and shades of gold.

Painting the forms of the hills, with the sketch layer hidden

Adding small brushstrokes to rough-in the cliff forms

Painting redder colors on the sky

5 **Painting the cliffs, beach, and sky.** Next, paint the cliff and hill forms in the middle ground. Continue to use the Gouache brush at a low opacity in Multiply mode when you want to paint transparent washes. Using brighter colors and slightly more contrast than you used for the distant hills helps to bring these landforms more forward in the composition. (I used more saturated purple and golden colors.) When painting the purples over the gold, you will see many variations of purples and browns, as the low opacity and the Multiply mode work together to "mix" the colors as you paint. When you'd like to paint with a semi-opaque paint, use Normal mode and a reduced opacity. (I used 30–40% opacity for these kinds of strokes, like the angled strokes shown in the left side of the image above). Often, I sampled color directly from the image (press the Alt/Option key to temporarily switch from the Brush tool to the Eyedropper) and then continued to paint with the brush.

Still working on the same layer, I added form and detail to the low-lying cliffs on the right side of the painting and to the beach. I also added red-orange color to the sky and carried it down onto the side of the taller hill.

In preparation for painting the grass in the foreground, I added a new layer and then used loose strokes while painting a medium-toned purple base color. Next, I painted deeper tones using darker purple colors. When painting the grass, keep your hand loose and make soft, curved strokes from the bottom to the top of each blade. To paint a thinner tip on the grass blade, reduce the pressure as you finish the stroke.

LEARN MORE ABOUT. . .

* adding a new layer. . . page 26
* saturation. . . page 42

The foreground blocked in, and the in-progress water

You can see the general highlights on the central boats.

6 **Painting the foreground details.** Now it's time to paint the water and add interest to the fishing boats. For the darker areas on the water, use the Gouache brush at a lower opacity in Multiply mode, as you did for the hills. When you add darker detail to the boats, you can also use the brush in Multiply mode.

To paint light color over dark when adding form and highlights to the fishermen and boats, use the Gouache brush in Normal mode. I used a small brush, between 5–7 pixels, and low opacities from 7–15% to paint soft details and highlights.

In areas where I had applied rougher brushstrokes, I used the Smudge tool to smear and blend them into the image (for instance, the blended strokes on the side of the cliff, and the foreground grass).

Now that the painting was nearly complete, I deleted the digital rough sketch layer and the scanned sketch reference layer (from step 1). I did not want to incorporate them into my image.

You can see the highlights on the left boat and detail on the water and grass, as well as the smudged and blended areas on the cliff.

The sunlight layer showing the active selection and the yellow fill

The sunlight layer with the blend mode set to Soft Light

7 **Adding the sunbeams and details.** Now that the landscape elements are modeled, it's time to enhance the focal point of your painting. My inspiration was the moment of sunshine bursting over the hill that illuminated the bay and the fishermen at sunrise. The sun rays help to enhance the focal point—in this case, the fishermen heading out in their boats.

To have the most flexibility when painting the sunbeams, add a new layer and position it at the top of the layer stack. Using the Polygon Lasso tool, make a selection as shown in the image above, and then give the selection soft edges by feathering it. Choose Select > Feather, and enter a value between 20–30 pixels. Now sample a light golden yellow from the sky using the Eyedropper tool, and fill your selection by choosing Edit > Fill, using Normal mode at 100%. To give your sunlight layer a subtle transparency, choose Soft Light from the Blend mode menu on the Layers palette. You might also want to experiment with the other blend modes.

The transparency effect was nice; however, I wanted to add more interest to the sunbeams. So I added a layer mask

to the sunlight layer and used a soft brush to paint long strokes on the layer mask to hide part of the sunlight layer.

To add a layer mask to your layer, click the Add a Mask button at the bottom of the Layers palette. Choose the Airbrush Soft Round 65 preset from the Brushes palette. Choose black, click on the Add Layer Mask button on the Layers palette, and paint on your mask (adjust the brush opacity if needed). Your image updates to show the area hidden by the mask. Working with layer masks is flexible and nondestructive to your painting. You can re-paint the layer mask until you have the sun rays as you like them. To bring more attention to the leading boat, I added a new layer and painted a few more small sun rays coming down in front of the boat.

Now step back and study your painting. Is there an area where you need more or less contrast? Do you see

LEARN MORE ABOUT. . .

* layer masks. . . pages 198, 207

The nearly final image showing the sunlight effect and the sunrays painted near the front boat

The final sunlight effect on the front boat

details you want to refine? After taking a good look at my painting, I used a small brush to add subtle detail to the fishermen in the central boat, and I defined some of the edges (on the "purples" layer). I also painted a few small sun rays around each boat on the "small sunrays" layer.

In this technique, you learned ideas for enhancing the focal point in your images. A Painter technique follows on the next page.

The details on the fishermen in the center boat

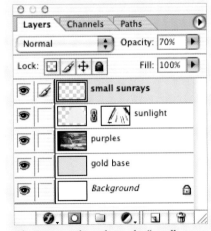

The Layers palette shows the layer mask on the "sunlight" layer selected. You can see the black paint on the layer mask, which hides part of the imagery on the layer.

The Layers palette shows the "small sunrays" layer selected.

The sunlight on the fishermen and boat

Along Tomales Bay

Strengthening the Focal Point in a Painter Image

Artist Pastel Chalk, *using various sizes and opacities*

Square Soft Pastel, *using various sizes and opacities*

Square Soft Pastel *strokes with* **Grainy Water** *used to blend, using various sizes*

ARTIST'S MATERIALS

Tablet: Medium-soft pressure

Program: Painter

Paper: Basic Paper

Paint: Colors chosen in the Colors palette or in the Mixer

Brushes:

• Artist Pastel Chalk: opacity and grain vary with pressure

• Square Soft Pastel: opacity and grain vary with pressure; strokes also change subtly, depending on the bearing (direction) of the stylus

• Grainy Water: the opacity of this Blender brush varies with pressure

The scanned colored pencil drawing of Tomales Bay

To paint *Along Tomales Bay*, I used a technique based on a traditional method of blended pastels. For inspiration, I used a colored pencil sketch done on location. To improve the composition, I made the image wider and extended the water ways. Also, I used a lighting filter to achieve an effect almost like a hole in a cloud, which would bring attention to the focal point. In the scene, the estuary streams converge, creating an interesting design that leads into the focal point area with the trees.

1 **Drawing and scanning.** Choose a sketch that you want to use as a reference for your painting. I drew the colored pencil sketch shown above in my 8 x 10-inch travel sketchbook. After scanning the drawing into Photoshop at actual size and at 300 pixels per inch,* I cropped the scan and adjusted its tonal range.*

LEARN MORE ABOUT. . .

* scanning. . . pages 90–91
* cropping an image. . . page 90
* adjusting tonal range. . . page 91
* using the Mixer. . . page 46

Using the Mixer to create a new color theme

Painting over the sketch with the Square Soft Pastel to build the underpainting

2 Building a color palette. You can sample color from your drawing if you like using the Dropper tool, or you can do as I did, and use different colors for your painting. I wanted to give my painting a cooler color theme than you see in my sketch, with cooler greens in the marshes, and lighter, cooler blues in the water and sky, like you might see in spring. The warmer colors in the sketch (for instance, the golden marshes) were the colors you'd see in the fall season. I used the Mixer palette to mix several colors to use for my color theme.

3 Painting over the sketch. Now you'll paint over your sketch with new color and create an underpainting using your sketch for a reference.* Put your sketch on a layer so that you can control its opacity. Next, make a new layer and position it above the sketch layer in the Layers palette. Choose the Square Soft Pastel variant of Pastels and a light blue color for the sky. Working on the new layer, use loose, expressive strokes to brush color onto the sky. To achieve atmospheric perspective

LEARN MORE ABOUT. . .

* underpainting. . . page 162
* value. . . pages 61, 75
* modulating color. . . page 138
* blending. . . page 138

(where faraway elements recede into the distance), choose a light blue gray, and brush it onto the distant hills. As you move forward in your composition, gradually use brighter color and more contrast.

 Underpainting. I often build an underpainting with base colors. I did that in this painting, with the blue-gray hills and the broad areas of greens on the trees and the marshes. Blocking in the basic colors gives me a good idea of how my composition is developing. I often refine elements at the underpainting stage. For instance, I changed the direction of a few of the waterways to improve the design.

The underpainting before adding more width to the image

After the canvas was increased, I painted in the side areas.

4 **Developing the underpainting.** Continue to lay in the basic shapes and colors for your composition. To improve my design, I refined the direction of the streams to make more pleasing curves that would lead the viewer's eye more gracefully into the focal point.

For larger areas, continue to use the Square Soft Pastel, changing the brush size as you work. For more detailed areas, switch to the Artist Pastel Chalk variant of Pastels. For the underpainting stage, I recommend using both brushes at their full opacity.

Now that the underpainting was complete and my composition elements were in place, I removed my scanned sketch from the file. If you no longer want your reference sketch, remove the layer from your image by selecting it in the Layers palette and pressing the Delete button (the trash can button on the Layers palette).

5 **Adding more canvas.** After you've completed your underpainting, take time to study your composition. At this point, I made a proof print and hung it on my studio wall to study. My composition seemed to need more tension, and I wanted to make the waterways leading into the focal point longer. If I made the length of the waterways more dramatic and moved the focal point (the area with the trees where the lines converge) to the left, it would create a more asymmetrical composition with more tension. Also, diagonals, like the waterways in this composition, are dynamic. To enlarge the image, I added more canvas size to the right side of the image (250 pixels), and I added a smaller amount to the left (50 pixels) to give more space to the tree on the left. Then I sampled colors of paint from the painting with the Dropper tool and painted in the areas to extend my composition.

If you feel that your composition can be improved by extending your canvas, select the Canvas layer and choose Canvas > Canvas Size, and enter the number of pixels that you want into the fields. You might need to experiment to arrive at the amount that is right for your image.

Using a low-opacity pastel brush to subtly modulate paint color

Blending the transitions between colors in the sky and on the hill

6 Blending and modulating color. Now that your underpainting is complete, it's time to add character and interest to the paint and blend areas that you want to soften.

My painting has several areas of color that may appear flat at first glance. However, the painting would be boring if these color areas were just one color. To add subtle interest, I sampled color from the image and changed it slightly, and then used a pastel brush with reduced opacity to apply the strokes. To modulate color in your painting, choose the Square Soft Pastel 20, and reduce its opacity to about 40% using the Opacity slider in the Property Bar. Sample color from your image with the Dropper tool, and change the value slightly using the Colors palette.* Now make short dabbed strokes, being careful not to cover the paint underneath completely. In areas where you want the effect of more shadow, use a slightly darker value, and in areas that are catching more light, use a lighter color.

You might want to soften the transitions between colors in your image. One of Painter's strengths is being able to blend and pull paint easily and expressively. Choose the Grainy Water variant of Blenders and experiment with blending areas of the sky. Pull from a darker area into a lighter area using your stylus. The opacity of the Grainy Water changes as you apply pressure to your stylus—if you apply more pressure, the opacity increases—and with less pressure the opacity is reduced.

In my underpainting, I had painted light- and medium-value blues and grayer blues onto the sky. To soften the colors and to suggest afternoon sunlight shining through wispy clouds, I used the Grainy Water blender.

Examine your image. Do you need to add details in the foreground or in the focal point areas? Will your image benefit from more contrast in the focal point area?

I zoomed into the area with the trees and used a small Artist Pastel Chalk brush to refine the edges of the tree shapes, and I made a few areas darker. I wanted a loose look, not a photo-realistic look. I also refined the irregular shapes in the tree foliage (the holes in the foliage), to make them more distinct. Then I emphasized some of the wavy lines on the edges of the waterways.

The modulated color and most of the detail are added in this image. This example is before adding the lighting effect.

You can see the soft lighting effect on this example. This image is before I painted into the lit areas.

7 **Using lighting to enhance the focal point.** To make the lighting and atmosphere in your image more dramatic, you can use Painter's Apply Lighting filter over your entire image or within a selected area.* Choose Effects, Surface Control, Apply Lighting. You can experiment by trying the lighting presets on your image and then choosing Edit > Undo (Ctrl/Cmd-Z) after each lighting effect that you apply. For an effect similar to mine, choose the Cool Globe light preset. This light has a cool, light blue ambient light color saved within the light

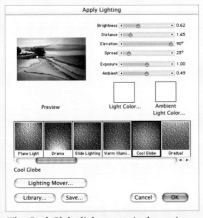

The Cool Globe light preset is chosen in the Apply Lighting dialog box.

that enhances the blue and green colors in your image. If you have a warmer color palette (such as reds, yellows, and browns), I recommend using the Warm Globe lighting preset. If you feel that the effect is too strong, you can always choose Edit, Fade to reduce the lighting effect.

Painter's Apply Lighting filter is intuitive to use, and when you use it with the subtle light choices (such as the Warm Globe, and Cool Globe lights), it produces natural results. To further integrate the lighting into your image, consider painting back into areas where the effect seems most obvious. For instance, I painted back into my image on the right and left sides of the marshes, in the foreground and on the sky. Sample color from your image using the Dropper tool and lighten or darken it slightly (depending on the color you want to rework), and then apply a few low-opacity brushstrokes to the areas. I used the Square Soft Pastel (in various sizes) to apply color and then blended the areas with the Grainy Water variant of Blenders. The final image is shown on page 134.

This technique demonstrates more ideas for enhancing the focal point in your images, including composition tips and using the Apply Lighting filter. Now you can take a break or move on to the next chapter.

Distribudor, Old San Jose

11

SIMULATING PAPER AND CANVAS

In this chapter, you'll learn ideas and methods for using texture in your images. In the first project, you'll use Painter's texture-sensitive Chalk brushes to paint an image with a bright color palette and a rich paper texture. Then you'll learn how to add more texture to your image using surface texture effects. For the second project, you'll create a painting in Photoshop using custom brushes—including one that reveals canvas texture—and learn more ideas for adding texture to your paintings.

 Distribudor, Old San Jose *was inspired by the quaint buildings in the old town of San Jose Del Cabo in Baja California. Years ago, when my family and I would travel through the town on our way to the surfing points on the East Cape, we would get sodas and beer at the Distribudor and fish tacos in the little blue building next door. I made several sketches of the colorful buildings in the area. I wanted to create a painting with a wild sky, almost as if a summer storm was coming. I chose a palette of colors that included earthy colors as well as bright oranges and purples, which would help to establish the dramatic mood.*

For Little Wolf *on page 148, I was inspired by the beautiful open space, cliffs, and hills near the ocean in Monterey, California. I painted a lonely figure walking alone in nature. For a warm look, I used a color theme of mostly golds, oranges, and browns with accents of blue, purple, and green.*

To finalize the compositions and to achieve the textured looks, I did a lot of experimentation with color, texture, and brushwork. In both paintings, I used techniques similar to those I would use with traditional tools.

Creating a Painter Image that Has Rich Texture

Blunt Chalk, *using various sizes and opacities*

Soft Oils, *with* **Grain Emboss** *texture added*

Blunt Chalk *strokes with* **Grainy Water** *used to blend, using various sizes*

The brown colored pencil sketch

ARTIST'S MATERIALS

Tablet: Medium-soft pressure

Program: Painter

Paper: Basic Paper

Paint: Colors chosen in the Colors palette or in the Mixer

Brushes:

- Blunt Chalk: opacity and grain vary with pressure

- Soft Oils brush: custom brush based on the Medium Bristle Oils variant of Oils; opacity and bristle marks vary with pressure

- Grain Emboss: the opacity of this brush varies with pressure

- Grainy Water: the opacity of this blender varies with pressure

For *Distribudor, Old San Jose*, I designed a composition that included interesting perspective on the buildings. Cropping the colored sketch enhanced the design and brought more attention to the buildings. Rather than follow every detail of the painting process, this technique focuses on the brush-stroke and texture application where possible. I chose to use the Chalk brushes because they would be helpful while painting the richly textured, time-worn masonry on the buildings.

LEARN MORE ABOUT. . .

* scanning and cropping. . . pages 90, 91
* putting a sketch on a layer. . . page 136

1 **Developing the composition.** To begin, make a conventional sketch and scan it,* or if you prefer, draw directly in Painter using the Cover Pencil variant of Pencils.

If you've scanned a drawing, put a copy of the image on a layer* so that you can lower the opacity of your reference and use it as a guide while painting.

If you sketch directly in Painter, open a new file and add a new transparent layer for your sketch, which allows you to adjust its flexibility.*

In this technique, I used a copy of the sketch on a layer for reference, and painted over another copy of the sketch on the Canvas. This way, I could leave part of the sketch showing if I wanted to, and use or discard the sketch on the layer depending on the development of the painting. After

The pencil study colored in Painter will become the underpainting.

The cropped and reworked composition

you've created your sketch, make a copy of the layer and then drop the copy to the Canvas by selecting it and choosing Drop from the Layers palette menu.

I drew the colored pencil drawing shown above on location in my 8 x 10-inch travel sketchbook. After scanning the drawing into Photoshop at 300 pixels per inch at actual size, I cropped the scan* and saved it as a TIFF file, which I opened in Painter. I put a copy of the sketch on a layer for safe keeping and turned off its visibility.

Working on the Canvas layer, I used the Cover Pencil and Painter's capability to draw straight lines to clean up the lines on the buildings. Pulling the straight lines also helped me to refine the perspective. Then I used the Blunt Chalk variant of Chalk to add color to the drawing, creating an underpainting using earthy colors, and blending paint with the Grainy Water variant of Blenders. The Grainy Water variant changes opacity based on pressure. To achieve subtle blending, press lightly on your stylus; to pull and blend more paint, apply heavier pressure. I painted a sky with wispy clouds, using richer colors. The images above show the sketch layer visible on

top of the in-progress underpainting. At this point, I merged the sketch with the Canvas by choosing Drop from the Layers palette menu.

As you work over your sketch, give thought to the design of your painting. Would enlarging the height or width or cropping help your design? I decided to crop the right side of my composition to strengthen the design to focus more attention on the perspective.

 Sketching with straight lines. You can use any brush to draw straight lines by enabling the Straight Line Strokes drawing option. Choose a brush (I chose the Sharp Chalk variant of Chalk), and click the Straight Line Strokes button in the Property Bar. To draw with freehand strokes again, click the Freehand Strokes button.

The Freehand Strokes and Straight Line Strokes buttons in the Property Bar (left) and the Sharp Chalk strokes (right)

Repainting the study with brighter color using a custom Soft Oils brush

Detail of the repainted area showing bristle marks painted with the Soft Oils brush

2 Adding bright color and textured brushwork. Now you'll use your colored sketch as a base to create the next stage of the underpainting. Choose your new Soft Oils brush from the Oils category in the Brush Selector Bar.* Using expressive strokes, paint over the colored drawing. In areas where you have verticals (like the windows and doors in my painting), take care to pull vertical brushstrokes. I used my stylus to pull from top to bottom. If you want a more perfect straight line next to a door, you might want to enable the Straight Strokes option in the Property Bar, and then consider breaking up the perfectly straight lines with a few well-placed freehand strokes so that it looks more natural.

 Making the custom Soft Oils brush. The Soft Oils brush is a brush with soft, coarse bristles that is based on the Medium Bristle Oils from the Oils category. To build the brush, open the Brush Creator (Window > Brush Creator). Choose the Oils from the category picker and the Medium Bristle Oils 25 from the variant picker. For a slightly irregular look to the bristles, set Jitter to .10 in the Property Bar (beneath the main menu). Now click the Stroke Designer tab, open the Bristle section, and make these adjustments to the sliders: Change Thickness to 54% for thicker bristles, set Clumpiness to 77 to make them clump together more, and set Hair Scale to 550% for denser bristles. For more variation in the thickness of the bristles, set Scale/Size at 30%. Now save your new variant by choosing Save from the Variant menu (above the tabs) in the Brush Creator. Before you close the Brush Creator, it's a good idea to restore the Medium Oils 25 brush to its defaults by choosing Variant > Restore Default Variant from the menu.

The Soft Oils settings in the Bristle section

Beginning to add chalk texture over the image. I blended areas of the sky using the Grainy Water variant of Blenders.

Detail showing the overlaid color and texture painted with the Blunt Chalk variant of Chalk

3 **Layering with chalk texture.** The most important concept is the layering of different textures. After the underpainting is as you like it, choose the Blunt Chalk variant of Chalk. As you use your stylus to paint with this Chalk, remember that light pressure produces more grainy strokes, and heavy pressure applies more paint and reveals less grain. While building up the layers of texture, try to preserve some of the brushwork you painted with the Soft Oils. As I worked, I varied the size of the Chalk. To finish, I added a few more strokes with a small Soft Oils brush on the road and the buildings and blended a few areas using the Grainy Water. On the next spread, you'll find more ideas for enhancing your Painter images with texture.

Detail showing the dabbed strokes in the sky and the subtle texture on the clouds painted with the Blunt Chalk variant of Chalk. The details on the trees were painted with a tiny Soft Oils brush.

Embossing Texture on an Image

In addition to the layering of oil and chalk brushwork that I used for *Distribudor*, you can use the Grain Emboss variant of the Impasto brush to "paint" three-dimensional textures on your images. I used two images and applied a single texture emboss to each one. This technique looks best if you do not paint texture equally over the entire image. The idea is to fool the eye.

Embossing a paper texture. Here you'll use a brush to paint a three-dimensional paper texture effect. Open an image you've painted using the Chalk, Pastels, or Oils Pastels brushes. (My image was about 1500 pixels wide.) Begin by choosing the Grain Emboss variant of Impasto in the Brush Selector Bar. For a subtle look, reduce the opacity of the brush to 30–50% in the Property Bar. To apply the paper texture effect like the image at the top right, choose Basic Paper in the Paper Selector. For more realism, keep the paper scale size (in the Papers palette) the same scale that you used when you painted the image. (I used 100%.) Apply gentle pressure as you emboss the texture. (I added it to a few of the foreground walls on the stucco buildings.)

Before using the Grain Emboss brush

After using Grain Emboss with paper texture

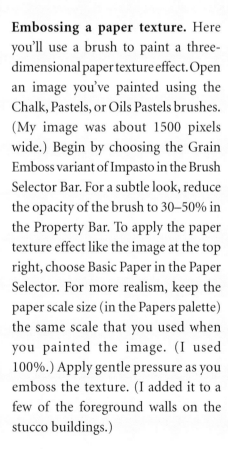

Before using the Grain Emboss brush

Embossing a canvas texture. This time, open an image that you have painted with the Oils or Acrylics brushes. (I used an earlier version of *Distribudor* painted with the Soft Oils brush (shown on page 144.) Choose a canvas texture in the Paper Selector.

After using Grain Emboss with canvas texture

Using your low-opacity Grain Emboss brush and gentle pressure, have fun applying the canvas texture to your image. I added canvas texture to a few of the foreground areas on the right side of the image.

Using Distortion and Surface Texture

You can use Painter's powerful Glass Distortion effect to bend an image, and use its versatile Apply Surface Texture effect to add realistic highlights and shadows to the image.

Before applying the two effects

After applying the distortion and surface texture

1 **Distorting the image.** Open an image that you've painted with an Acrylic, Gouache, or Oils brush. First, you'll "bend" the image based on its luminance by choosing Effects > Focus > Glass Distortion. Experiment with the values. You need higher settings for larger images. (My image measured about 1500 pixels wide.) I set the Using menu to Image Luminance, the Map menu to

Refraction, and chose Good Quality. I increased the Amount to .20 and left the other settings at their defaults.

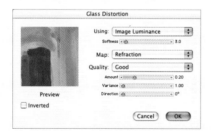

The Glass Distortion dialog box

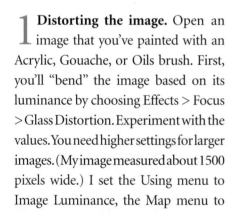

Using paper texture. You can use the Glass Distortion and Apply Surface Texture filters to apply Paper textures in addition to the Image Luminance effect that I've demonstrated here. In the Using menu of both dialog boxes, choose Paper, leaving the other settings the same. Have fun experimenting!

The image after applying Glass Distortion

2 **Applying texture.** Now choose Effects, Surface Control, Apply Surface Texture. In the dialog box, set the Using menu to Image Luminance, Amount to 15–20% (for a subtle look), Shine to 0% (for a matte finish), and experiment with the Light Direction buttons. (I chose the lower-left button.)

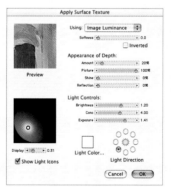

The Apply Surface Texture dialog box

Like magic, you have thick paint! Now you can take a break or move on to the next technique.

Little Wolf

Achieving Texture in a Photoshop Image

Airbrush Soft Round, using various sizes

Tapered Spatter, using various opacities

Gouache, using various opacities

Gouache, showing textured dry brush effect

The brown colored pencil drawing

The painting *Little Wolf* is composed of a sketch and loose dabs of color, with the only detail being the lone figure on a path to the hills and the dramatic sky. This technique doesn't show every step of the painting in great detail, but focuses on a variety of texture application ideas.

I based the technique on a favorite method of using transparent watercolor and gouache, and used bright colors and loose semitransparent dabs of color. To paint the figure, I used tiny brushes and more contrast to bring him into sharper focus.

1 **Setting up.** Choose a sketch that you want to use as a reference for your painting. (I drew the pencil sketch shown above in a 5 x 7-inch travel sketchbook.) After scanning the drawing into Photoshop at actual size and at 300 pixels per inch,* I adjusted its tonal range.* Now put the sketch on a layer (in Multiply mode, and with a reduced opacity) so that you can keep the drawing and color elements separate.*

LEARN MORE ABOUT. . .

* scanning. . . pages 90–91
* adjusting tonal range. . . page 91
* putting a sketch on a layer. . . page 93

Paint dabs for a new color theme

Painting with the Airbrush Soft Round and a Spatter brush to build the underpainting

2 **Building a color palette.** You can sample from the Color Picker as you go, but I recommend planning your basic color theme before jumping into your painting. Most of the warm colors in my painting were golden oranges and warm greens that you'd see in the autumn season. Because the landscape was relatively simple, I chose to use rich color and a lot of contrast in the sky. The purples in the sky would complement the oranges, because they were opposite one another on the color wheel. I used the Spatter brush and my stylus to paint dabs of color for a color palette.

3 **Painting translucent washes.** Choose a color from your color palette or from the Color Picker. You can paint your basic colors on the Background or on a new layer set to Normal mode. (For this image, I chose to paint my first washes directly on the image Background.) Now choose the Airbrush Soft Round 65 preset from the Brushes palette (set the Painting Mode to Normal), and paint soft wispy clouds, starting by blocking in the darker colors first. Then choose lighter colors and use gentle pressure on your stylus to paint the lighter clouds.

To add the look of falling rain to the sky, choose the custom Tapered Spatter brush that you made in

Chapter 8. Reduce its opacity to about 30% in the Options Bar, and using a light pressure on your stylus, pull long, sweeping strokes down to suggest the rain showers. The bristle marks on the sides of the brush give the effect of rain.

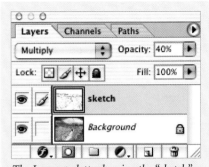

The Layers palette showing the "sketch" layer active and set to Multiply mode, and at 40% opacity

The final color study created with the Airbrush Soft Round, Spatter, and custom Gouache brushes, before adding the canvas texture effects

You can see the dry brushwork on the path in this detail.

4 **Completing the loose study.** Continue to develop your color study. Apply broad areas of color using the Gouache brush (set to Normal mode), focusing on the larger shapes first, and then come back into areas and gradually add details, as you come forward in your composition. I added subtle details in the foreground grass, but used colors with similar values. To focus attention on the figure, I used more contrast and a tiny Gouache brush to paint details. For the dry brush texture on the path and the cliffs in the foreground, I used my custom Gouache Dry Brush.*

 Building the custom Gouache Dry Brush preset. This brush appears to be "dry" because of the texture saved within the brush and because each "tip" is textured. To build it, begin by choosing the Gouache brush that you built in Chapter 9. Turn on the Texture check box and open the Texture section of the Brushes palette. From the Pattern menu, choose Extra Heavy Canvas and click the Invert button (for a drier look). Now set the Scale to 35, set the Mode menu to Color Burn, and enable the Texture Each Tip check box. Next, enable the Shape Dynamics check box so that the stroke thickness changes based on pressure. Save your new brush by choosing New Brush Preset from the Brush palette's main menu. (I named my brush Gouache Dry Brush.)

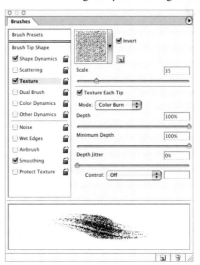

The Texture section of the Brushes palette

In these detail images, you can see the canvas texture.

5 **Adding a subtle canvas texture.** When you're adding a textured effect to your image, always remember that it's best to do so to fool the eye; apply the effect subtly, because too strong of an effect will look fake.

For *Little Wolf,* I applied texture to a layer, and then used a transparent blend mode to composite it into the image.

Begin by adding a new layer to your image. Target the layer, and then choose Edit > Fill. In the Fill dialog box, set the Use menu to Pattern, set the Mode menu to Normal, and set the Opacity to 100%. From the Custom Pattern menu, choose Extra Heavy Canvas, and click OK. You will see the new layer fill with the canvas texture.

Now set the Blend menu in the Layers palette to Overlay to composite the texture with your image. For more creative fun, consider experimenting with the other Blend modes—especially Soft Light and Color Burn—as they also work well with textured effects. For a subtle, natural look, I reduced the opacity of the texture layer to 21%. For the final image, I set the sketch layer to an opacity of 40%. Turn the page to see the completed final image, and two creative sidebars that feature more solutions for adding canvas textures to your images.

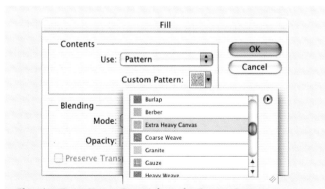

Choosing Extra Heavy Canvas from the Custom Pattern menu

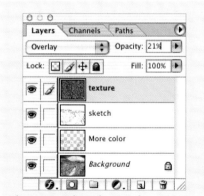

The Layers palette showing the settings for the "texture" layer

Adding Texture with the Texturizer Filter

In addition to the method that I used for my *Little Wolf* study, there are more ways to add texture to your images in Photoshop; for instance, you can use the Texturizer filter on your image.

Before applying the Texturizer filter

After applying and compositing the texture

1 Setting up a layer. In this exercise, you'll use the Texturizer filter for a coarse weave look. Open the version of a painting that has not had texture applied. You can apply the Texturizer filter directly to your image, but you will have much more control over the effect if you set it up on a layer. Now add a new layer that is filled with 50% gray by choosing Edit > Fill. (The Texturizer filter will not work on a layer that has empty pixels.) In the Fill dialog box, set the Use menu to 50% Gray, set the Mode menu to Normal, and set the Opacity to 100%.

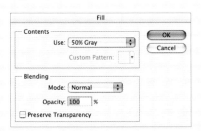

The settings in the Fill dialog box

2 Simulating a burlap texture. Now choose Filter, Texture, Texturizer. When the dialog box appears, choose Burlap from the Texture menu, and experiment with the Scaling and Relief sliders if you like. I wanted a coarse look, so I left scaling at 100%. For a realistic look set the Relief slider to 4.

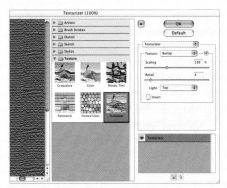

Setting up the Texturizer dialog box

3 Blending the texture with the image. When you have your texture as you like it, composite your texture layer with the image by choosing the Overlay mode from the Blend menu on the Layers palette. (You can experiment with other Blend modes; for instance, Soft Light produced a nice result with this layer.) For a more subtle texture look, I reduced the opacity of the layer to 42% in the Layers palette.

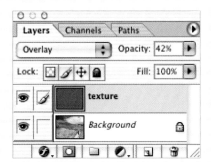

The Layers palette showing the Blend mode and opacity settings

Adding Texture with the Lighting Effects Filter

You can apply a canvas texture to your image using a lighting effect and a texture channel, as shown in this example, which uses another version of the *Little Wolf* painting.

A version of the Little Wolf *study before applying the lighting effect*

1 Creating a texture channel. By putting texture into an alpha channel in the Channels palette, you make it accessible to the Lighting filter. Open an image that has no texture added to it yet, and add a new channel to the image. Select the channel in the Channels palette, and then choose Edit > Fill. In the Fill dialog box, set the Use menu to Pattern, set the Mode menu to Normal, and set the Opacity to 100%. From the Custom Pattern menu, choose Extra Heavy Canvas, and click OK. You'll see the new channel fill with the texture. I used the default channel name of "alpha 1."

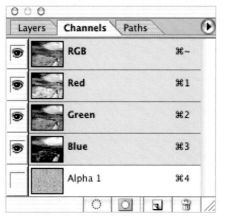

The new channel "Alpha 1" is filled with the texture.

2 Copying your image to a layer. Now that your texture channel is set up, copy your image to a new layer by choosing Select > All, and from the Layer menu, choose New > Layer Via Copy. Keep the new layer selected.

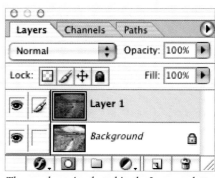

The new layer is selected in the Layers palette.

A new version of the Little Wolf *study after the lighting effect was applied*

The paint seems to melt into the texture in this close-up view.

3 **Applying the lighting effect.** Now choose Filter, Render, Lighting Effects. In the Lighting Effects dialog box, choose the Omni light from the Light Type menu. Set Intensity to 39. Under Properties, set the Gloss slider to –97, Material to –100, Exposure to 7, and Ambience to 8. Now set the Texture Channel menu to Alpha 1. Next, enable the White is High check box, and set the Height to about 30.

4 **Finessing the look.** A textured lighting effect can appear artificial on an image, so I recommend adjusting the layer Opacity and Blend mode for a more pleasing, natural look. For a subtle effect of pigment melted into canvas, I chose the Soft Light Blend mode and settled on an Opacity of 50%.

Congratulations! In this chapter you learned how to apply texture with brushes and special effects.

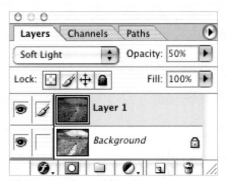

The Layers palette with settings

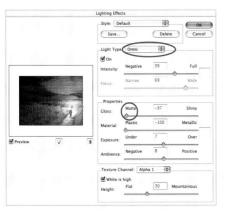

The Lighting Effects dialog box with settings

The image with lighting effects applied

The lighting effects blended with the image

Downstream Path, Summer

12

MIXING MEDIA

You'll enjoy using several kinds of digital media in this chapter, and you'll learn ideas and methods for combining the new media in innovative ways. In the project, you'll use Painter's incredible Impasto to "gesso" a canvas. Then you'll use Oil brushes to rough out an underpainting using a bright color palette. Next you'll layer grainy pastel and thick paint over the top using your stylus, without losing the interesting texture underneath. Photoshop users can take these artists' processes and methods and incorporate them into that program, using custom brushes that simulate watercolor, oil, and chalk. The results can be pleasing, but they are not identical.

 Downstream Path, Summer *was inspired by a favorite location in San Diego, California. I wanted to create a painting that had the feeling of a clear, hot sunny day, with wispy clouds that would allude to a coming weather change. I chose a palette of colors that included warm, earthy colors on the cliffs and varied turquoise blues for the clear sub-tropical ocean. The complementary colors would work together to create an inviting painting. In this painting, I left no area of the canvas with a flat look. To add varied texture to the oil painting on canvas, I added touches of grainy pastel on the beach and sea foam. I finished by adding a few details with thick Impasto paint.*

Painting with Oil, Pastel, and Impasto Paint on Canvas

Flat Oils and Medium Bristle Oils strokes

Square Hard Pastel stroke

Thick Bristle, Palette Knife, and Distorto Impasto strokes, using various sizes

ARTIST'S MATERIALS

Tablet: Medium-soft pressure

Program: Painter

Paper: Coarse Cotton Canvas

Paint: Mix color using the Mixer

Brushes:

• Flat Oils and Medium Bristle Oils: strokes change based on pressure and the bearing (direction) of the stylus

• Square Hard Pastel: opacity and grain change based on pressure and stroke changes with the direction of the stylus

• Thick Bristle, Palette Knife, and Distorto Impasto: thickness of the paint and stroke width change based on pressure and the bearing (direction) of the stylus

This colorful conventional felt tip marker sketch inspired my colors and composition.

For *Downstream Path, Summer,* I designed a composition that emphasizes the solidity of the cliff forms and the perspective. To focus attention on the cliffs and water, I set the horizon about one-third of the way from the top of the canvas. I saw the cliffs as large topographic blocks moving back and the water's softer curves as the ideal complement to these more solid block forms of the cliffs.

Rather than follow every detail of the painting process, this technique will focus on the composition process and of creatively mixing media to resolve the work.

1 Designing the composition. To begin, make conventional sketches and scan them, or if you prefer, draw directly in Painter using one of the Pencils variants.

If you've scanned a drawing, cut the image to a layer* so that you can lower the opacity of your reference and use it as a guide while creating your underpainting and reworking the composition.

LEARN MORE ABOUT. . .

* scanning a sketch. . . pages 90–91
* putting a sketch on a layer. . . page 136
* adjusting tonal range. . . page 91
* using the Mixer. . . page 46

The tighter pencil sketch shows more detail in the forms.

This colored pencil sketch inspired the activity in the water and sky.

If you choose to sketch directly in Painter, open a new file and add a new transparent layer for your sketch. Drawing on the layer gives you more flexibility with how you incorporate your sketch into the image.

I began this landscape by drawing a tight sketch and a few color studies. This process helps me to get the scene and its forms ingrained in my mind. That way when I complete the painting in my studio, I can pull from my memory, because I took the time to truly observe and study my subject.

I drew the pencil, felt tip marker, and colored pencil studies shown here on location in my travel sketchbook. I scanned the tight pencil sketch, opened it in Painter, put it on a layer, and set the Composite Method to Multiply. I named my layer "sketch."

On the two following pages, you'll see a sidebar "Building a Gessoed Canvas," which describes how I set up a colored ground (with a canvas texture and gesso) for the painting.

Continued on page 162

Composing a landscape. Although the location I've used here is spectacular, you don't always have to look for such a perfect setting for a successful painting—it's possible to derive inspiration from any scene. Look for a good composition in a series of hills, trees, or in elements from any landscape. Frame the space by making a rectangular frame with your hands, and look for a good design. You can also get a sheet of paper and cut a rectangular or square hole in it, and use the hole to frame your viewing.

You can draw or paint any subject and make it interesting if the composition is good. A simple composition can be intriguing if it is composed dynamically with interesting angles and curves and a strong focal point. Areas of loose brushwork activity with energy in the brushstrokes and an interesting atmosphere do wonders for a simple scene.

Building a Gessoed Canvas

In Painter, you can set up a gessoed canvas on which you can enjoy painting with a variety of media, including pastel, oil paint, and thick Impasto paint.

Detail of the embossed canvas

Detail of the gessoed canvas

1 Making a colored ground. Open a new file with a cream colored background. (My file was 3300 x 1950 pixels, at 300 ppi. The size of the file affects the appearance of the texture.) If you find performance on your computer slow when using Impasto on a file this size, you can use a smaller file, such as 1500 x 1000 pixels.

To set the Paper Color, click the Paper Color preview in the New window and choose a color in the Colors dialog box. To choose a new hue or adjust its saturation, click or drag in the color wheel. To make the color darker or lighter, adjust the value slider on the right side of the window. When you have a color that you like, click OK to accept it.

2 Embossing the canvas. Now you'll brush a canvas texture onto the image surface for the look of evenly gessoed canvas. Choose a rough canvas texture from the Paper Selector. (I used Coarse Cotton Canvas.) For more flexibility, make a new layer for your embossed canvas and name it to keep your image organized. (I named mine Gessoed Canvas.) Choose the Impasto brush category in the Brush Selector Bar, and then choose the Grain Emboss variant. If you are using a file size similar to mine, scale the brush up to about 140 pixels. Using a light, even pressure on your stylus, gradually brush the texture onto the image surface.

To give a more subtle canvas effect, I adjusted the Surface Lighting. Choose Canvas > Surface Lighting, and reduce the Amount to 80% and the Shine to 20%.*

3 Painting thicker gesso. To add more interest to your embossed canvas, add some thick paint. Choose a Thick Bristle variant of Impasto. For the look of thicker paint, increase the Depth to about 20% in the Impasto section of Brush Controls. (Choose Window > Brush Controls > Impasto, or choose Window > Show Brush Creator and click the Stroke Designer tab and the Impasto tab.)* Using varied pressure on your stylus (and the same cream color you used for your colored ground), add brushwork to your canvas. For a realistic gessoed look, I suggest not covering the entire canvas, but using well-placed brushstrokes to add interest. * Allowing the strokes to overlap occasionally provides a rich look. I suggest using a soft touch to avoid completely covering the embossed canvas texture.

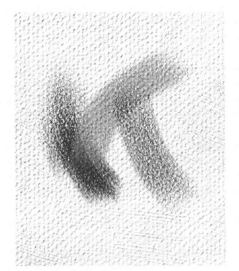

Square Hard Pastel brushstrokes

Flat Oils brushtrokes

Thick Bristle and Palette Knife brushstrokes

4 **Trying out brushes**. You can achieve a variety of different media effects on your gessoed canvas. The first two brushes described here apply thin paint to the canvas, without adding thick (impasto) paint that covers the gesso texture. For more flexibility, make a new layer for your paint, and then choose the Pastel category and the Square Hard Pastel variant. (Keep the same Coarse Cotton Canvas loaded that you used to create your canvas.) Hold your pen at an angle, and make a few relaxed strokes using varied pressure. The Square Hard Pastel stroke changes based on the angle

LEARN MORE ABOUT. . .

* Surface Lighting. . . page 167
* Impasto. . . page 167
* a gessoed canvas. . . pages 160–161
* loading a paper library. . . page 39

and direction of your hand and the pressure that you apply. Applying less pressure also reveals more grain; applying more pressure covers the valleys in the paper grain.

Now choose the Oils category and the Flat Oils variant. This brush responds to the pressure you apply and to the angle and direction of the stylus as you paint. Make a few relaxed brushstrokes, and notice the thin wash of paint on the canvas.

The next brush that you'll try out applies thick, Impasto paint to your gessoed canvas. Choose the Thick Bristle variant of Impasto, and make a few expressive brushstrokes using varied pressure. Next, choose the Palette Knife variant of Impasto, and reduce its size to about 10 pixels. Using heavy

pressure, make a few strokes into the paint you applied with the Thick Bristle. You'll notice that the Palette Knife excavates, or digs into the thick paint. The knife is also useful for scribbling interesting marks into the gesso. I used the Palette Knife to scrape and move paint on the foreground cliff face of *Downstream Path, Summer* on page 156. When you've finished trying out the brushes, you can delete this layer by dragging it to the trash can on the Layers palette.

 A gessoed canvas. When working with conventional materials, I often apply a coating of paint to the canvas to add texture and to seal the ground so that it absorbs less paint during the painting process.

Painting on the gessoed canvas using the pencil drawing as a guide

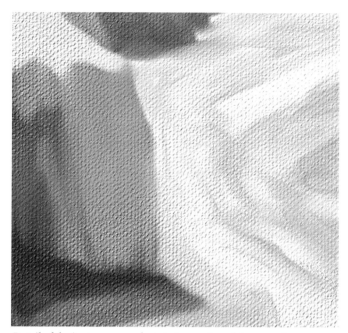

Detail of the in-progress underpainting on top of the gessoed canvas

2 **Creating an underpainting.** For more flexibility, make a new layer to hold your underpainting, and name it. Next, you can mix your colors using the Mixer.* If your painting will depict the bright sunlit day like mine, mix light, warm, saturated colors. Then to work out the color and value relationships in your painting, begin by painting broad areas of color for an underpainting. (So that it would not be distracting while I painted, I lowered the opacity of the pencil drawing layer to about 30%.) To apply the first washes onto the Underpainting layer, use the Flat Oils or Medium Bristle Oils variants of Oils. You can experiment with the other Oils brushes, but at this point, I recommend staying away from using the brushes with "Thick" in their name because they apply Impasto paint. (You'll use Impasto brushes later in step 5.)

LEARN MORE ABOUT. . .

∗ using the Mixer. . . page 46

∗ Impasto. . . page 167

As a painting develops, I constantly rework areas and refine the composition. The pencil drawing was important to help me remember structure, but I did not let it restrict my brushstrokes when I needed to change the shape of one of the cliffs or paint looser edges.

 For Photoshop users. If you don't have Painter, you can follow along with this technique in Photoshop. See the instructional sidebar on page 44 on how to load the brushes. Use the custom Sketcher brush from page 116 for the sketch; then for the oil painting, try the Tapered Spatter brush described in Chapter 8 on page 92 or the Gouache Dry Brush in Chapter 10 on page 117. For the grainy strokes, try the Dry Media Brushes, such as the Pastel Rough Texture and the Soft Pastel Large. (These brushes are useful and fun to paint with, but they do not produce identical results to the Painter brushes.)

The underpainting of the cliffs, sky, and beach is nearly complete in this image.

Color inspiration and interpretation. The golden afternoon light reflecting off the ocean cliffs on a clear sunny day was my inspiration for the color palette. I love the use of Impressionist color. Rather than toning down the color for my shadows using black to give the illusion of atmosphere and depth, as a colorist, I find ways to enhance the natural richness found in reflected light on my study's surfaces. During the development of the painting, I looked at my earlier color studies and visited the location again in afternoon sunlight to make more color notes for the lighting on the cliffs and beach. You can take a photo for reference, but often a photo does not record all of the impressions that you can see. While looking at the color in nature, I relax. Then, to simplify the forms and see larger areas of color, I squint and gaze at the area to see the subtle colors of the reflected light coming from the beach onto the cliffs. Try not to think about the details in the landscape when analyzing the color because this can cause you to miss important but subtle variation in the colors. The colors you use in a painting help to set the mood and evoke the emotion of the work.

The in-progress painting with the sketch layer hidden

Painting the planes and forms of the cliffs

3 Building more complex color and form. When you're satisfied with the underpainting, move onto resolving your composition. When my underpainting was complete, I hid my sketch so that it would not distract me. (Click the sketch layer eye icon closed to hide the layer.)

For more flexibility, add a new layer to hold your new paint. (I named my layer "paint.") In the Layers palette, enable the Pick Up Underlying Color check box. Using the Flat Oils and the Medium Bristle variants of Oils (in various sizes), paint brushstrokes to sculpt and refine the forms progressing from the back of your composition (farther away) to the mid-ground and foreground. The Flat Oils brush is ideal for blocking in the planes of the cliffs and for laying in broad areas of color on the water and sky. The Medium Bristle is a round brush that changes size and opacity subtly depending on the pressure you apply. I customized this brush so that it would paint strokes of more varied thickness.* Then I used this

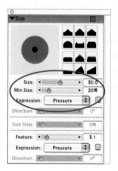

A more tapered brush. You can customize the Medium Bristle Oils to paint sensitive thin-to-thick strokes based on the pressure you apply, similar to the way a conventional round brush performs. Select the Medium Bristle Oils, and then open the Size section of the Brush Controls (Window > Brush Controls > Size). (Size is also in the Stroke Designer within the Brush Creator.) Make sure that the Size Expression is set to Pressure, and then set the Min Size to 20%. In the Spacing section (Window > Brush Controls > Spacing), reduce the Spacing to 9% and Min Spacing to .05%. To save your new variant, choose Save Variant from the pop-up menu on the Brush Selector Bar, and give it a name. I named my brush Tapered Medium Bristle. Now return the default Medium Bristle to its original settings by choosing Restore Variant from the pop-up menu.

Painting varied gold strokes on the cliffs with the Medium Bristle Oils

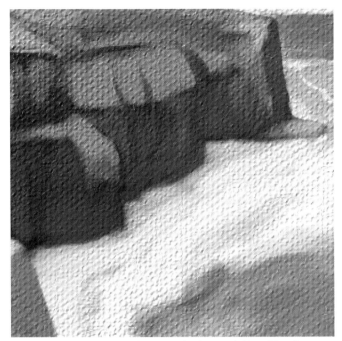

The in-progress color modulation on the distant cliffs and beach

brush to refine edges and to paint linear details (for instance, the wavy blue brushstrokes where the waves spill onto the beach).

To help the faraway landforms recede into the distance, I recommend using less contrast than you'll use in the foreground. Instead of painting the shadows using high contrast in this seascape, I chose to use moderate contrast and to modulate the shadows with varied color. For the details in the shadows, I used subtle changes in color, with warm and cool purples and blues. Where the sun was brightest on the cliffs, I painted vibrant golds and oranges and warm browns.

The evolving painting. Continue to work over your painting; relax and respond to your design and color as the image develops. Experiencing a dialogue with the painting is a wonderful sensation for an artist. As you work, let your painting evolve. At some point, you'll begin to look at your references less and respond to the paint as you make decisions. If the balance of the painting calls for brighter hues in the water than you'd originally planned for, go ahead and experiment by painting with the brighter colors on a new layer. You'll be able to control the strength of the color by adjusting the opacity and the composite method. I continually compose and rework the composition throughout the painting process. Sometimes it's as if the painting takes on a life of its own.

LEARN MORE ABOUT. . .

 saving custom brushes. . . page 37, 164

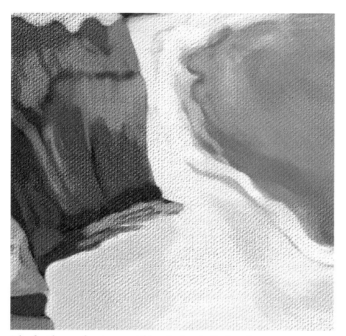

The first layer of grainy pastel brushed onto the beach

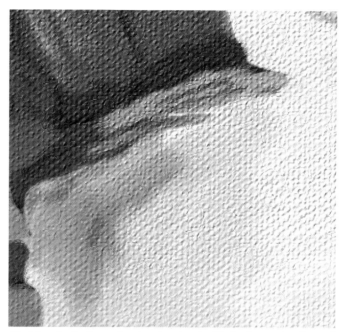

Modulated color in sand on beach painted with the Square Hard Pastel

4 **Painting grainy pastel for texture interest.** You learned several ideas for enhancing the focal point of a painting in Chapter 10. Using the right combination of mixed media can also help to strengthen the center of interest. Now that your painting is nearly complete, take the time to look at your composition. Are there areas that would benefit from more or less contrast? Where do you need to refine details? Are you satisfied with the feeling of atmosphere and mood in your painting?

To achieve a subtle layering of texture, you can paint with grain-sensitive brushes over the oil paint on canvas. The grainy brushes are ideal for simulating the look of sand or to achieve the look of sparkling light reflecting from the sea foam. This mixed media technique would be very messy if you combined oil paint and pastel traditionally. Painter and the computer give you the ultimate in flexibility. For the most realistic texture effect, choose the Coarse Cotton Canvas texture in the Paper Selector. Choose the Pastels brush category and a Square Hard

Pastel variant. As you paint with the Square Hard Pastel, you'll notice that the opacity and grain vary with pressure and that the strokes also change subtly, depending on the bearing (direction) of the stylus, as you work.

To create interesting layered texture on the beach, begin with broader strokes in a color just a little bit darker than the existing paint. Apply the pastel using a light touch to allow more texture to show. In areas of shadow, mix a few colors that are a little darker and brush lightly to apply them over the top. Be careful not to completely cover the texture underneath.

I continued to add touches of grainy pastel using the media to add color and texture interest on the breaking waves and on the beach in the foreground. I also added grainy strokes of light golden yellow to the clouds to carry the sunny warm color theme into the sky.

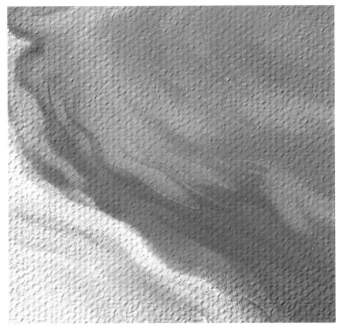

Using the Distorto Impasto brush to pull paint at the water's edge

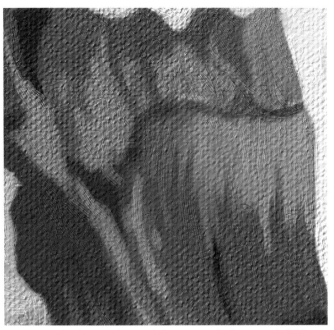

Using a small Palette Knife to work the paint on the foreground cliff face

5 Adding expressive details with thicker paint. Make a new layer to hold the thicker Impasto paint, and then choose the Impasto category and the Thick Bristle variant. As you rotate your hand and tilt the stylus toward you, the bristles of this brush spread out on the far side of the brushstroke. The width of the brushstroke and the opacity of the paint also changes based on the pressure you apply. As you work over an area, the paint builds up more thickly. To scrape back into an impastoed area, use the Palette Knife (Impasto), and use heavier pressure to carve into existing Impasto paint. I recommend reducing the size of the Palette Knife to 5–10 pixels and using the brush to move smaller areas of paint. To push and pull paint with a more pointed tool, try the Distorto Impasto. I used this brush to add a swirly look to the waves. When you're using your stylus and the Distorto Impasto to push and pull paint, the paint moves like wet oily paint. To finish, I added a few more touches of thick paint to the cliffs and water. You can see the entire completed painting on page 156.

 Impasto appearance. Two features control the height and depth of Impasto: the Depth setting of individual brushstrokes (located in the Impasto section of Brush Creator) and the Canvas > Surface Lighting dialog box, which controls the global appearance of Impasto.

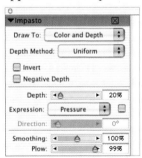

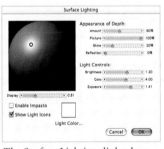

The Impasto section of Brush Controls with Depth set to 20% for an individual brush

The Surface Lighting dialog box includes settings for the appearance of the Impasto for the entire document.

In this chapter, you've learned ideas for mixing media with your images. Now you can take a break, or move on to the next chapter.

Wanda, 1945

13

RETOUCHING, TINTING, AND PAINTING

This chapter has two parts. In the first section, you'll use the Clone Stamp tool in Photoshop and your stylus to eliminate scratches and other problems from a photo. Next, you'll add a few subtle tints to the image and create a vignette border. In addition, you'll learn how to make a custom History brush preset in Photoshop so that you can use your photo as a source for a painted study.

In the second section, you'll create a rich paper surface in Painter and use Painter's powerful cloning features to add painterly interest to the image using brushwork that complements the forms. In addition, you'll use the Artists' Oils—a new medium in Painter—to paint a portrait based on a photo.

A vintage photo of my mother, Wanda, provided me with inspiration for Wanda, 1945. *I liked the warm, aged sepia look of the photograph, so I worked to preserve this color throughout the development of the image. I used Photoshop's efficient Clone Stamp, brushes and selection tools, and my Wacom tablet and stylus to retouch the photo and add a vignette. For* Wanda 1945, Study *on page 178, I wanted a more textured look, so I built a light-colored paper surface in Painter and used that program's cloning features and brushes to paint over the clothes, hair, and background, taking care to preserve the important features in my subject's face. For the photo-painting* Afternoon Self Portrait *on page 186, I wanted to create the look of an oil painting. The Artists' Oils and a tiny Palette Knife allowed me to apply colored paint, and blend the paint with imagery from the photograph.*

Retouching and Adding a Vignette

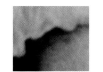

Clone Stamp Pressure, *various sizes*

Airbrush Soft Round, *65 pixels, Normal and Color modes*

The scan of the vintage photo

ARTIST'S MATERIALS

Tablet: Medium pressure

Program: Photoshop

Paint: Sampled information from the image and colors from the Color Picker

Brushes:
- Clone Stamp Pressure: ideal for subtle retouching; opacity is controlled by pressure on the stylus
- Airbrush Soft Round, various sizes: flow of paint is based on pressure on the stylus

Inspired by the warm, aged sepia look of the photograph of Wanda, I wanted to preserve the color throughout the development of the image. Using favorite Photoshop features, I retouched the photo, brightened the subject's eyes and teeth, and added a few subtle color tints to the image. To complete the look, I added a soft vignette.

1 **Selecting a subject.** Choose a black-and-white or color portrait photo without a cluttered background, and with good detail. Your digital photo or scan should be in RGB mode and should measure about 1800 x 2500 pixels.* Before you start the retouching process, save a new version of the image to work with and preserve the original just in case you want to start over.

Retouching in Painter. If you do not have Photoshop, you can follow the retouching process in Painter. The Lasso tool, Select, Feather command, and layers operate similar to the functions in Photoshop. You can perform point-to-point clone repairs in Painter using the Soft Cloner in much the same way that you can in Photoshop with the Clone Stamp. In addition, Painter offers useful retouching tools in the Photo brush category, such as the Scratch Remover brush and the Saturation Add brush, in addition to the Dodge and Burn brushes. All of these brushes are already set up to work well with a pressure-sensitive tablet and stylus.

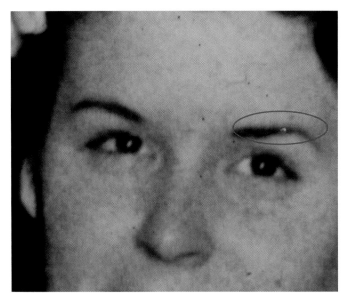

The scratch on the right eyebrow

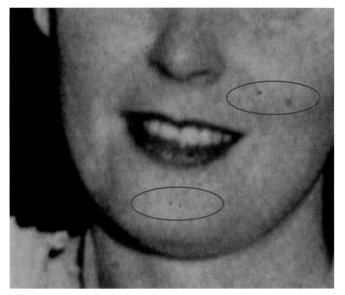

The dirt spots on the cheeks and chin

2 Analyzing the subject and setting up. To begin, use the Zoom tool to magnify your image, and analyze the areas that need repair. If you've chosen a vintage photo, your subject might have scratches and spots of dirt. To repair these areas, I recommend using a custom Clone Stamp that changes opacity based on the pressure you apply to the stylus. (You can also use the Healing Brush, but the Clone Stamp was a better choice for my subject with freckles.) The directions for building this custom Clone Stamp are described in the "Retouching using pressure" sidebar on this page. After you've built the brush, I recommend using it with the Normal Painting mode.

Before beginning, it's a good idea to copy your photo to a new layer so that you can control the opacity of the retouching edits if needed. Simply drag the Background layer over the Create a New Layer button on the Layers palette, and a new layer will appear in the layers list.

LEARN MORE ABOUT. . .

* scanning. . . pages 90–91

Retouching using pressure. Using this special Clone Stamp, you can repair images with more finesse and control because the opacity of the tool is based on the pressure you apply to your stylus. Begin by choosing the Clone Stamp tool. From the Brushes palette, choose the Air-brush Soft Round 45 preset. Now enable the Other Dynamics check box in the left side of the Brushes palette, and in the Other Dynamics window, set the Control menu under Opacity Jitter to Pen Pressure. Then save your new Clone Stamp tool preset by choosing New Tool Preset from the Tool Preset Picker menu in the Property Bar.

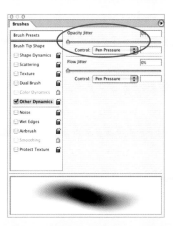

Setting Opacity to Pen Pressure in the Other Dynamics window

A detail of the image before the repair

You can see the retouched eyebrow, cheeks and chin.

3 **Sampling and repairing.** To repair a dirt spot or a scratch, you'll want to use the Clone Stamp to sample a similar but clean area near the area you want to repair, and then apply the sample information to cover the spot. Carefully choose an area that is the same tonal value and color of the area surrounding the problem area so that the repair will be "seamless." Press Alt/Option. (You'll see a cross-hair cursor appear.) Now, click to sample from the clean area, and release. Then click on the area you want to repair. (You might need to adjust the size of your brush tip as you work.) Be careful not to scrub the area

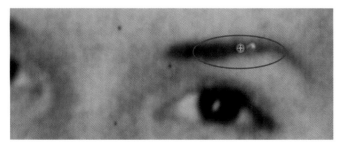

When you press the Alt/Option key, you see the Clone Stamp cursor. Here, I am sampling information from the eyebrow.

as you apply the new information, but click with the stylus. If you drag or scrub with the Clone Stamp, you will build up an undesirable repeated pattern.

To repair my subject's eyebrow, I scaled the brush tip smaller. To ensure that I would build up paint gradually, I set the Opacity slider in the Property Bar to about 30%. Then I used gentle pressure and a steady hand to apply the sampled pixels to repair the scratch on the eyebrow. I repeated the process to repair the dust spots on the face, while being careful not to completely paint over the freckles on the woman's face.

 More useful retouching tools. In addition to the tools used in this project, Photoshop offers more retouching tools that work well with a pressure-sensitive tablet, such as the Dodge, Burn, and Sponge tools, and the Healing Brush. You can create your own pressure-sensitive presets for each of these tools, in much the same way that you created the pressure-sensitive Clone Stamp on page 171.

The soft-edged selection for the eyes

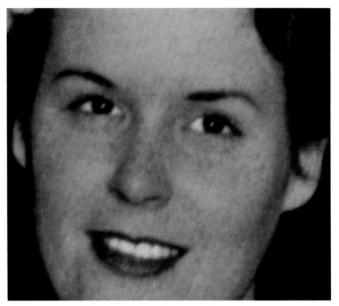

The eyes and teeth are brighter in this example.

4 **Brightening the eyes and teeth.** Now that you've repaired the scratches and dirt, you might want to focus more attention on the eyes and teeth by lightening them. First, analyze your image. If the photo is sepia or gray, do the whites of the eyes and the teeth look muddy or have too much tone? I recommend brightening them subtly so that your correction will not stand out too much. I used the Levels dialog box to adjust the light areas of the eyes and teeth.

Begin by making a freehand selection of the whites of the eyes using the Lasso tool and your stylus. Draw a selection for the left eye, press the Shift key to add to your selection, and draw the selection for the right eye. Now give your selection a soft edge by choosing Select > Feather and typing a value in the field. (For my 1800-pixel-wide image, I used a 5-pixel feather.) Just in case you might need it later, save your selection as an alpha channel in the Channels palette by choosing Select > Save Selection. (I named my alpha channel "eyes.") To make the tonal adjustment, choose Image > Adjust > Levels, and in the dialog box, drag the Input Levels High-

lights slider a little bit to the left. This will take some of the tone out of the lighter areas of the eyes, while preserving the highlights and shadows on the forms. If the effect is too strong, you can always choose Edit, Undo and try again.

When you're happy with the eyes, use your stylus and the Lasso tool to draw a freehand selection for the teeth, and follow the same process you used for the eyes to save the selection and to brighten the teeth. (I named this alpha channel "teeth.") I made these adjustments separately because the eyes and teeth in my image needed different highlight adjustments.

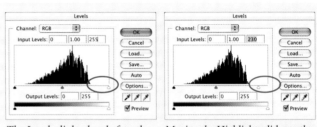

The Levels dialog box before the adjustment   *Moving the Highlights slider to the left to lighten the teeth and eyes*

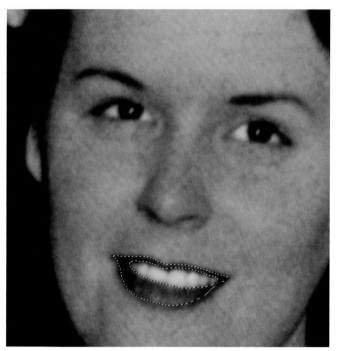

You can see the active freehand selection in this image.

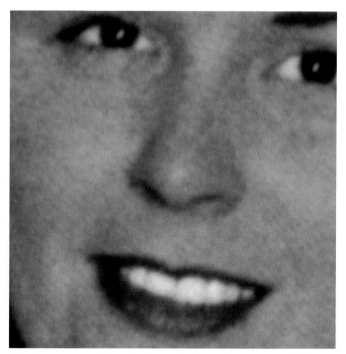

Painting the color tint on the lips, with the selection marquee hidden

5 Coloring the lips and details on the clothes. If your subject is a woman, you might want to add a color tint to her lips. Begin by making a copy of the retouching layer for editing flexibility. (I named my new layer "color tints.") Then make a selection to constrain the paint. Using the Lasso tool and your stylus, draw a selection border around the outside edge of the lips. You can use the selection you saved for the teeth to protect them during the tinting process as follows. With the new selection for the lips active, choose Select > Load Selection, and when the dialog box appears, choose the "teeth" channel from the Channel menu, click the Subtract from Selec-

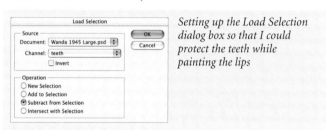

Setting up the Load Selection dialog box so that I could protect the teeth while painting the lips

tion button, and click OK. Your selection should look similar to the above left image.

When the selection is as you want it, hide the selection marquee so that you can focus on the painting. (Press Ctrl/Cmd-H to hide your selection marquee.) Now choose the Brush tool and the Airbrush Soft Round 45 preset. In the Color Picker, choose a color that will complement your image—make sure that it is not too bright or saturated—so that you will achieve a subtle result. In the Property Bar, set the Painting Mode menu to Color, and choose a reduced opacity for the airbrush. (I used 30% opacity.) Then use your stylus to gradually build up a soft color tint on the lips.

For your image, you might choose to add colored tints to all of the clothes, or to color just a few details, as I did. I added subtle yellow tints to the flower and to the blouse, following the same selecting and tinting process used for the lips. After your tinting is complete, save a new version of your image before moving on to the next step.

A detail of the image with the tints

The oval selection on the image

The vintage portrait with the soft vignette

6 **Adding a vignette to the image.** A soft vignette adds elegant style to your portrait. Begin by making a copy of your "color tints" layer, and name your new layer "vignette." Next, make an oval selection around the subject using the Elliptical Marquee tool. For a soft edge, choose Select > Feather. (I used a value of 30 pixels for my 1800-pixel-wide image.) Save your vignette selection in the Channels palette in case you need to use it later. With the feather in place, choose Select > Inverse to select the area outside the original oval boundary, and then clear this area by pressing Backspace/Delete. Next, make a new layer and fill it with white to help show off the vignette, and drag this layer directly below the vignette layer. Good work! You have retouched and tinted your image, and you've created a beautiful vignette on your photo.

Now save the image in Photoshop format, which preserves the layers and alpha channels, in case you want to make changes to one of the layers later. Now that the

retouching, tinting, and vignette steps are complete, you are ready to move on to the next phase of the project.

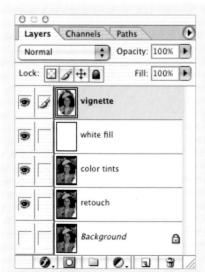
The Layers palette shows the retouch, color tints, vignette, and white fill layers.

Painting with History in Photoshop

You can use your stylus with the History brush tool in Photoshop to create paintings from your photos. Although the process is not as intuitive as painting from a photo in Painter, you can achieve some pleasing results.

The vintage portrait with the soft vignette

The Background copy layer at 30% opacity

1 **Setting up layers.** To begin, open the portrait you retouched earlier in this chapter in Photoshop and make a copy by choosing Image > Duplicate. Merge the layers with the Background by choosing Flatten Image from the Layers menu. Save the new file in TIFF format. (You can begin with a layered file for this technique, but to make the process easier to follow, it's best to start with a flat file.)

Now you'll make the layers for the technique to give you editing flexibility. Make a copy of the background layer by dragging it over the Create a New Layer button on the Layers palette. Set the opacity of the Background copy layer to about 30%. Then add an empty new layer directly below it and

fill this new layer with white. This layer "hides" the original on the Background. Finally, add an empty new layer, and give it a unique name. (I named mine "chalk.")

The Layers palette is set up for using the Background copy layer as a low-opacity reference while painting.

2 **Painting with history.** Select the Background layer, and open the History palette (Window > History). Choose New Snapshot from the History palette menu. In the New Snapshot dialog box, choose Current Layer from the pop-up menu.

Next, choose the "chalk" layer. Then choose the History Brush tool, and in the Brushes palette, choose the Chalk preset with the 36-pixel tip from the default brush preset list. Save your new tool preset for later use by choosing New Tool Preset from the Tool Preset Picker on the Options Bar. (I named my new preset "History Brush Chalk.")

Using the Background copy layer as a guide while painting with the History Brush Chalk

The final study with the Background copy layer hidden

You can see the chalky texture in this detail.

Next, in the History palette, set the source for the History Brush to Snapshot 1, which allows you to paint using information from this snapshot.

The source is set to Snapshot 1 in the History palette.

Using your stylus and the History Brush Chalk preset, begin to lay in brushstrokes. Concentrate on making strokes that follow the direction of the forms, rather than scrubbing with your stylus or making the brushstrokes in just one direction. Imagine that you are sculpting the forms, as you did when you worked through the modeling exercises in Chapter 5, "The Illusion of Volume," even though you are working from a photo. The opacity of the "History Brush Chalk" is controlled by the pressure that you apply to your stylus. You'll also notice the appearance of more grain if you apply less pressure. I painted the face at nearly full opacity to showcase the portrait. For a casual vignette look, you might want to make looser strokes and apply less pressure to vary the opacity of the strokes on the edges of the hair and clothing, as I did. In areas where I wanted brighter color than the source image provided, I switched to the Brush tool. Using the default Chalk preset, I painted deeper yellow strokes on the flower, varying the size of the brush as I worked. To brighten the eyes and teeth, I used the Brush tool and a tiny Chalk brush to carefully paint lighter color on the teeth and the eyes.

I added more warm yellow colors to the flower corsage.

Wanda, 1945, Study

Working Over a Portrait with Chalk

Soft Cloner

Square Chalk, *varied sizes and opacities*

Square Chalk Cloner, *varied sizes and opacities*

Square Chalk, *smudged with* **Grainy Water**

The portrait retouched in Photoshop

ARTIST'S MATERIALS

Tablet: Medium-soft pressure

Program: Painter

Paper: Basic Paper: a versatile, medium-grain texture

Paint: Sample color from the image, and choose color in the Color Picker

Brushes:

• Soft Cloner: opacity varies with pressure

• Square Chalk: opacity and grain vary with pressure

• Square Chalk: modified to use Clone Color; opacity and grain vary with pressure

• Grainy Water: opacity and grain vary with pressure

1 Setting up. Painter offers realistic natural-media brushes and textures, which you can use with your photo images, and when painting "from scratch." To begin, open the portrait you retouched in Photoshop earlier in this chapter—in Painter— and flatten it by dropping the layers. Save the flat file in TIFF format. (You can open a layered Photoshop file in Painter, but to make the technique easier, I recommend starting with a flat file.)

To add brushwork to the image, you'll use cloning in Painter.* Make a clone of the TIFF file by choosing File > Clone, save the clone image, and give it a meaningful name that will help you keep your files organized. In this technique, you'll clear the clone canvas, create a paper surface, and then paint the photo back into the clone image. This process is useful when you want to achieve an irregular edge on a portrait. Now delete the contents of the clone canvas by choosing Select > All and Backspace/Delete. On the next spread, you'll see a sidebar that describes how to build a rich paper surface in Painter.

Powerful, intuitive cloning. Painter offers easy-to-use cloning features that allow you to sample source imagery and apply it from the source image to a destination image or from one point to another on a single image. You can use most brushes in Painter as cloning brushes by enabling the Clone Color button on the Colors palette.

Building a Rich
Paper Surface

Working with rich textures is one of Painter's most exciting features. You can create a colored paper surface to sketch and paint on or to clone imagery into. For the most realistic look, it's important to keep the texture at the same scale when applying the effects and brushwork.

The image with Color Overlay texture applied

Choosing a texture. Rather than clone the image into an empty white Canvas, you can set up a paper surface and then paint in more interest and background color using brushstrokes. Simply choose a texture from the Paper Selector. (I used Basic Paper texture because its versatile medium grain works well with Painter's chalk and pastel brushes.) For this effect, you might want to increase the size of the paper texture, based on the size of your image. For my 1800-pixel-wide

image, I scaled Basic Paper to 150% in the Papers palette. If the Papers palette is not open, choose, Window > Papers.

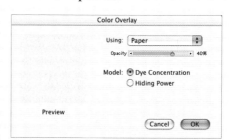

Scaling the paper in the Papers palette

LEARN MORE ABOUT. . .

* making a new layer. . .page 34

Applying a colored texture. Next, add a subtle colored texture to the background. Choose Effects > Surface Control > Color Overlay. In the Color Overlay dialog box, choose Paper from the Using menu. (I settled on an amount of 40% and clicked the Dye Concentration button.) Dye Concentration produces a more transparent result, whereas Hiding Power is semiopaque. I recommend experimenting with both options.

Applying Color Overlay using Paper

The image with Apply Surface texture added   *Applying chalk strokes over the rich paper surface*

Adding highlights and shadows. Now that you have the colored texture in place, it's time to give your paper surface realistic highlights and shadows. Choose Effects > Surface Control > Apply Surface Texture, and in the dialog box, set the Using menu to Paper. I recommend using a subtle Amount

setting between 10–30% for a more realistic look. (I used an Amount of 12%.) For this technique, you'll want a matte surface, so reduce the Shine setting. I set Shine at 0%, and left other settings at their defaults. It's fun to experiment with the Light Direction buttons to see which one best complements your image.

 Surface effects on a layer. The texture you applied with the Color Overlay and Apply Surface Texture effects can be covered over by paint or edited with an eraser. Because of this, I often paint or clone imagery onto a layer above the surface. You can also blend the texture layer with transparent composite methods (blending modes) such as Multiply or Gel.

Adding brushstrokes. If you'd like to add more interest to your image background, consider applying background brushwork before you begin to clone or paint. I recommend adding a new layer to your image for these background brushstrokes.*

Textures work well on layers as well as on the image Canvas in version Painter 8 and later. I wanted to add a more casual, textured look to my image, so I used the Eyedropper tool to sample a light brown color from the vignette image. Then I chose a large Square Chalk variant of Chalk and painted loose strokes over much of the background. To maintain realistic texture, keep the scaling of the Paper texture the same size that you used when applying the effects.

Adding subtle surface texture

Cloning the image with Tracing Paper enabled *The image with Tracing Paper turned off* *The cloned image, ready for the paint strokes*

2 **Painting the photo into the image.** Before you begin to clone the photo into your image, add a new layer to your file.* Then choose the Soft Cloner variant of Cloners in the Brush Selector Bar. The opacity of the Soft Cloner changes based on the pressure that you apply to the stylus. You might need to increase the size of the Soft Cloner and reduce its opacity to about 10% to

cover a large area smoothly. I set my brush size to 380 pixels in the Property Bar for this 1800-pixel-wide image. Enable Tracing Paper (Canvas > Tracing Paper) so that you can see your subject as you import it into the file. Beginning with light pressure, I carefully painted the subject's face solidly into the clone, and then added softer, lower-opacity edges

around the subject. I did not follow the oval vignette in the example, but created an irregular edge that showcased the hair, hat, and shoulders. It's a good idea to toggle Tracing Paper off and on as you work, so you can see how much of the actual image is coming in. With Tracing Paper enabled, it can be challenging to see the true tone and color.

LEARN MORE ABOUT. . .

* building a paper surface. . . page 180
* adding a new layer. . . page 34

The first textured strokes on the hat feathers and hair

The simplified forms on the crinkled hat material

3 **Adding textured brushwork.** Now that you've painted the focal point of the portrait into your clone image, it's time to add textured brush work. For more realistic texture, you'll want to keep Basic Paper chosen in the Paper Selector, and use the same scale you used when building the paper surface.* In this step, you'll paint brushstrokes on the hair, clothes, and background using color imported from the clone source photo. Make a new version of the Square Chalk 30 variant that you can use for cloning using the instructions in the "Making a grainy chalk cloning brush" sidebar.

As you use the Square Chalk Cloner, pay careful attention to the direction of the forms. Take care not to scrub or paint strokes in only one direction. My subject had curly hair, and this inspired me to paint short, curved strokes using my stylus. The feathers and the crinkled material on the hat provided more opportunities.

I painted short, dabbing strokes with my stylus, focusing on the more important planes to simplify the shapes in the crinkled hat material.

 Making a grainy chalk cloning brush. You can set up the Square Chalk to sample color from a clone source while you paint. Choose the Square Chalk variant of Chalk from the Brush Selector Bar. In the Colors Palette, click the Clone Color button (the Stamp). Using Clone Color allows you to paint with the Square Chalk and import color from the source image. Save your new brush by choosing Save Variant from the menu on the right side of the Brush Selector Bar, and give it a unique name. I named my brush "Square Chalk Cloner." Finally, for good Painter housekeeping, return the original Square Chalk variant to its default settings by choosing Restore Default variant from the Brush Selector Bar menu.

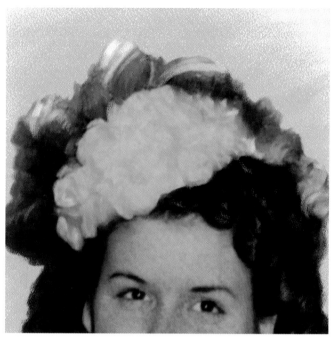

More highlights added on the hair and hat

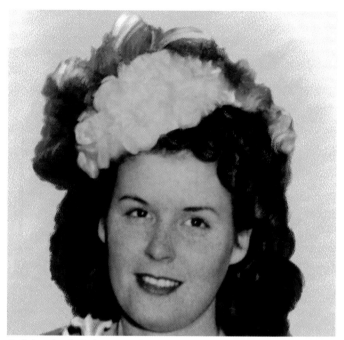

Refining the dark shapes on the hair

4 **Blending areas on the hair, hat, and clothes.** In areas where detail is not important, you can use the Grainy Water variant of Blenders to simplify and smooth areas of the cloned photo and to subdue the chalk texture if you feel it is too strong. Making these kinds of judgements helps the design of the portrait and makes it more unique. For instance, simplifying the shapes in the hat focuses more attention on the woman's face.

The opacity and grain of the Grainy Water are affected by the pressure you apply to the stylus. If you apply less pressure to the stylus, you will reveal more texture; if you apply heavier pressure, you'll notice the blending will be smoother, with less texture. To refine overall shape and texture of the hair, I used the Grainy Water to blend the edges of the hair.

LEARN MORE ABOUT. . .

＊ form and volume. . . pages 62–65

5 **Painting more grainy strokes.** After blending, I switched to the Square Chalk Cloner brush. Using gentle pressure, I applied grainy strokes to the edges of the hair and to the highlights on the curls. In areas where I wanted brighter highlights, I switched to the Square Chalk and used a lighter color to brighten them. I did not apply a lot of expressive brushstrokes to the face because I wanted to preserve the integrity of the portrait. When painting over the forms on your subject, imagine that you are sculpting the forms. Let your stylus and brushstrokes follow the direction of the forms.

The final brushwork on the hair and hat

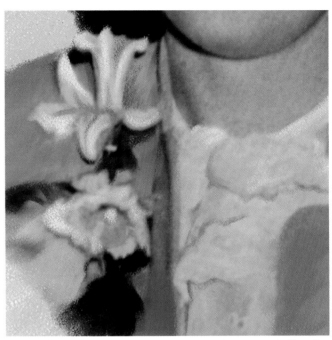

Adding yellow brushstrokes to the flowers with the Square Chalk and the blended ruffles on the blouse

6 **Adding final touches.** Take a careful look at your image. What details need to be refined? To finish, I used the Square Chalk to apply yellow color to the flower and lighter colors to the blouse. Then, using the Grainy Water, I blended a few areas on the blouse to simplify the ruffles and focus more attention on her face. I also added more light brown brushstrokes to the "paint" layer using the Square Chalk.

Congratulations! You've learned how to use Painter's powerful cloning features, how to make a cloning brush, and more! Now you're ready to move on to the next technique.

Blending edges on the hat

The final Layers palette

Afternoon Self Portrait

Painting a Portrait Using the Artists' Oils

Wet Brush brushstrokes

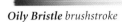

Oily Bristle brushstroke

Artists' Oils strokes with *Palette Knife* strokes used to blend, using various sizes

ARTIST'S MATERIALS

Tablet: Medium-soft pressure

Program: Painter

Paper: Artists' Canvas

Paint: Colors sampled from the photo or from the Colors palette

Brushes:

• Wet Brush: size varies with pressure

• Oily Bristle: size varies with pressure; grain varies subtly with pressure

• Oil Palette Knife: size varies with pressure

• Tiny Smeary Knife: opacity of this flat tool varies with pressure

The scanned portrait photo

To create *Afternoon Self Portrait*, I used the Artists' Oils—a new medium in Painter—to paint over a reference photo. Using a different work flow than earlier in the chapter, I laid in large areas of wet paint directly over a clone of the photo. To improve the composition, I simplified the background and added colors that would focus on the face. For more interest in the background, I modulated the background color and used interesting curves and angles in the brushwork. For smoother brushwork on the face and for details in the hair, I used tiny palette knives from both the Artists' Oils and the Palette Knives brush categories.

1 Selecting a photo, scanning, and cloning. Choose a photo with good lighting and contrast to use as a reference for your portrait painting. My subject had dramatic side lighting that would add interest to the portrait. My original photo measured 1200 × 1600 pixels. Adjust the tonal range* of your photo in Photoshop or Painter, if needed.

In Painter, make a clone of your image* and name it. I named my clone Portrait Retouch to keep my version files organized.

LEARN MORE ABOUT. . .

* adjusting tonal range. . . page 91
* making a clone. . . pages 179, 183

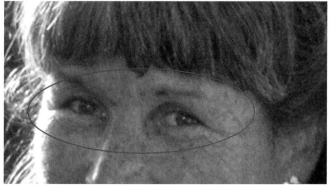

Before retouching the overly bright catchlights (above) and after (below)

Strokes painted with the Dry Bristle, Wet Brush, and Oil Palette Knife

2 **Retouching the image.** Take a good look at your image. Are there areas that you would like to improve by retouching? You can do the retouching in Photoshop or Painter, as described earlier in this chapter. Working on the clone image, I used a tiny airbrush to subdue the overly bright catchlights in the eye. I wanted a natural look, so I left the rest of the image as it was. To retouch, zoom in, and use the Eyedropper to sample color from a nearby not-so-bright highlight. Then use a tiny Fine Detail Airbrush (Airbrushes) to paint over the highlights. Save your retouched image, and then make a clone of it and name the new clone version. (I named mine Portrait Study 1.) Keep the retouched image open so that you can import color and imagery from it as you work on your portrait.

3 **Painting and blending with the Artists' Oils.** A new medium, the Artists' Oils let you apply wet oily paint and blend pigment just like traditional wet oil paint. The Artists' Oils are ideal for painting from scratch or for working over photos because of the medium's unique blending capabilities. Choose the Artists' Oils in the Brush Selector Bar, and the Oily Bristle variant. Use your stylus to paint a brushstroke. You'll notice that the Artists' Oils brushes run out of paint like a conventional brush. To apply new color with each brushstroke, lift the stylus and then replace it on the tablet when you make a new stroke. To blend existing color (or the pixels in your reference), do not lift the stylus, but continue to brush back and forth with the Artists' Oils. For more blending options, experiment with the Blender Palette Knife, Oil Palette Knife, and Wet Oily Palette Knife variants.

Painting over the background with the Artists' Oils

Working over the image with the Artists' Oils and an Oil Palette Knife

4 Simplifying the background. You can focus more attention on the face and improve the composition of a portrait photo by reducing the clutter in the background. Working directly on the image canvas, I used the Wet Brush and Oily Bristle variants Artists' Oils to apply oily paint and smear it over the background. Laying in the background first also helps to refine the design and brings the subject forward in the composition.

You can turn on Clone Color in the Colors palette to paint with color from your retouched photo, and you can sample color from the working image using the Eyedropper.

I chose to paint on the canvas to take advantage of the Artists' Oils feature that the entire canvas is covered with oil. The oily feeling is less noticeable when painting on a layer. For more information, see the sidebar on page 190.

5 Painting the hair. Now that the background is laid in, paint brushstrokes that follow the general shapes in the hair using a small Oily Bristle brush. Then use a smaller Oily Bristle brush or a tiny Oil Palette Knife (Artists' Oils) to repaint the area. To paint thinner strands of hair or to smooth over the skin, you can also use the Tiny Smeary Knife variant of Palette Knives. Applying strokes using a light pressure allows you to apply low-opacity paint and blend. Let your brushstrokes follow the growing pattern in the hair.

The Clone Color button is enabled in the Colors palette.

The broader strokes painted with the Oily Bristle brush on the highlights

The thinner brushstrokes painted with a Tiny Palette Knife

If you overwork an area and want to start over, you can switch to the Soft Cloner variant of Cloners temporarily to bring the details back.

As you can see, I painted broader strokes to lay in the shapes and values on the hair (and to cover the photo pixels). Then, using varied pressure on my stylus, I layered sensitive, thinner strokes over the top that would suggest the individual strands of hair using the Tiny Smeary Knife.

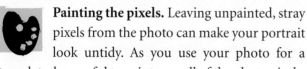 **Painting the pixels.** Leaving unpainted, stray pixels from the photo can make your portrait look untidy. As you use your photo for a template, be careful to paint over all of the photo pixels. You can zoom in to 200–300% and use the Grabber Hand to pan around as you examine your image and then touch up the unpainted pixels with a small brush.

 Painting on a layer with the Artists' Oils. If you prefer painting on a layer instead of directly over the cloned photo, you can do so using the Artists' Oils, but the paint will have less of an oily feel. Make a new layer, and in the Layers palette, enable the Pick Up Underlying Color button. Using Pick Up Underlying Color allows you to pull color from any layers and the Canvas below and mix it with new color you paint on the layer. When you apply the Artists' Oils brushstrokes to the layer, oil is applied within the Artists' Oils brushstrokes.

The Layers palette with Pick Up Underlying Color enabled

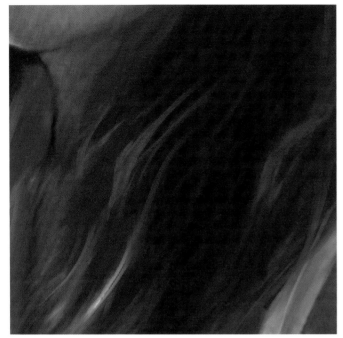

The loose brushstrokes on the hair painted with the Tiny Palette Knife

The in-progress sculpting of the face

6 Modeling the face and painting details. As you examine the forms and planes of the face, remember the form and value studies that you painted in Chapters 5 and 6. The human form can be simplified into cylinders, spheres and cubes, and so on. Pay careful attention to the highlights and shadows on the facial forms, because these lighting transitions reveal the forms.

To work out the skin tone colors, you can sample color from the working image, or from the retouched photo by enabling Clone Color for a particular brush and then painting. I recommend using the Oily Bristle brush and a small Oil Palette Knife (Artists' Oils) to paint over most of the skin. As you paint, let your brushstrokes follow the direction of the forms and planes of the face. While carefully paying attention to the lighting, I sculpted the rounded forms and planes of the face using the Oil Palette Knife and the Blender Palette Knife.

To add activity and interest to the portrait, I used looser brushwork on the hair and clothing, but I painted the face

more realistically because it is the center of interest. To emphasize the nose highlight, I used a small Oily Bristle brush and my stylus to paint a fairly straight brushstroke down the nose to widen the highlight. Then I strengthened the highlight on the side of the face using this brush.

For smoother areas of the skin, switch to the Palette Knives category and to the Tiny Smeary Knife. Zoom in and use this tiny brush to touch up areas on the face. To preserve the natural freckled skin, I lowered the opacity of the Tiny Smeary Knife to about 20% in the Property Bar.

For the teeth, I began by sampling color from a light area on the teeth. Then I lightened it a bit more in the Colors palette, and applied the lighter color using a low-opacity Tiny Smeary Knife. I also used this technique to brighten the whites of the eyes. To finish, I modulated color in the shadows and blended the shirt collar. You can see the final image on page 186.

Now that you've completed this photo-painting technique, you're ready to move on to the next chapter.

Where All Creativity Comes From

14

COMPOSING FROM THE IMAGINATION

This chapter reviews some of the techniques taught in earlier chapters, such as enhancing the center of interest with lighting and using traditional scanned sketches to start a painting. It carries these concepts further to build a more complex composition. This chapter has four parts. In the first section, you'll draw digital pen-and-ink sketches using Painter. In the second section, you'll use Photoshop to lay out a composition using the Painter sketches and scanned drawings. In the third section, you'll open the composition in Painter and add rich, colored brushwork (including painting wet-into-wet) with Digital Watercolor and atmosphere with a custom lighting effect. In the final section, you'll take the image back into Photoshop, where you'll build a layer mask that will hide areas of the light layer, including painting on the layer mask with your stylus and large brushes.

 Where All Creativity Comes From *was inspired by a wonderful dream. When I searched my library of sketchbooks for ideas, I came across the drawing of lilies, which gave me a concrete direction. To depict the scene of an angel bringing inspiration to the artist, I used a stylized approach that incorporates colored washes and pen drawings. To guide the eye around the illustration and tell the story, I designed a circular composition with the drawings. Then, using transparent washes of Digital Watercolor that would support the black-and-white ink drawing elements, I painted the elements. Near the end of the process, I used a lighting effect to enhance the mood and to help unify the composition.*

Sketching Art Elements in Painter

Croquil Pen strokes

Croquil Pen strokes with Tapered Eraser strokes

ARTIST'S MATERIALS

Tablet: Medium-soft pressure

Program: Painter

Paper: French Watercolor paper: a medium-grain texture

Paint: Black chosen in the Colors palette

Brushes:
- Croquil Pen: size and grain vary with pressure
- Tapered Eraser: size varies with pressure

Using a photo for reference while drawing

For *Where All Creativity Comes From*, I used a Croquil Pens brush in Painter to sketch most of the black-and-white drawing elements—the artist, easel, and angel. I'd already drawn the lily sketch with a fine-point marker in my conventional sketchbook, so I brought it into the composite file later as a scan.

Take time to look though your sketchbooks and references and choose a strong element that will inspire you to design the illustration.

 Slow performance? If you have a low-powered computer and the brushes seem to paint slower when you use several layers with a 50 MB-plus file, you can build your drawings in individual files and then paste them into the final composite as layers.

1 Making a digital pen drawing. Begin by deciding what size your final composition will be. (My file was 9 x 14 inches at 300 ppi.) Create a new file using the dimensions you need for your composite.

First, obtain a reference. (I used a digital photo.) Open your file, and copy and paste it into the new file that will become your composite. In the Layers palette, reduce the opacity of the reference layer, and use the Layer Adjuster to position it. Add a new transparent layer directly above the reference to hold your drawing. Set Brush Tracking; then using a Croquil Pen variant of the Pens and your stylus, make your drawing. I used the sketchy-line style*, because this style would go well with the scanned drawings that I planned to add later.

The pen drawing of the artist

The color study of my easel

The artist and the easel

2 **Adding to the drawing.** One of the most wonderful benefits of working on the computer is the flexibility to import elements from multiple sources. (As a reference for the easel drawing, I used a color study that I'd painted for another project.) This time, use the File > Place command to import the image into the composite file. (The Place command brings the image in onto a new, named layer in Painter.) Lower the opacity of the reference, position the second reference, and then add a new layer. Sketch as you did in step 1. If you need to touch up an area of your drawing, use a Tapered Eraser (Erasers). When you've completed your drawings, save the file in Photoshop format to preserve the layers. On the next spread, you'll open this working file in Photoshop. Remove the reference layers when your drawing is complete.*

Controlling the opacity of your references. You can build your own "digital lightbox" and simulate Painter's Tracing Paper feature by putting your references on layers and lowering the opacity of the reference layers. You can set up a reference like this one using Painter or Photoshop.

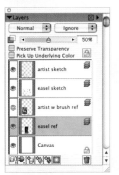

The Layers palette showing the easel ref layer at lower opacity (left), and how it appears in the image (right)

LEARN MORE ABOUT. . .

* Brush Tracking. . . page 52
* sketchy-line style. . . pages 55–56
* layers. . . page 34

The sketch composition for Where All Creativity Comes From

Compositing Sketches and Scans in Photoshop

The drawing of the artist created in Painter

The scanned drawing of the white lilies

ARTIST'S MATERIALS

Tablet: Medium pressure

Program: Photoshop

Paint: Sampled information from the image

Brushes:
• Clone Stamp Pressure: ideal for subtle retouching; opacity is controlled by pressure on the stylus

LEARN MORE ABOUT. . .

★ scanning. . . pages 90–91
★ the Clone Stamp. . . page 171

You can perform this stage of the project in Photoshop or Painter. I'm using Photoshop for this stage to demonstrate the portability between the two programs.

I opened the layered sketches file created on the previous spread in Photoshop. I wanted to combine it with a traditional drawing that was scanned and touched up in Photoshop.

1 **Assembling elements.** In the previous spread, you sketched in Painter. Now choose a sketch from your conventional sketchbook that you'd like to combine with your drawing done in Painter, or use pencils and paper to create a new drawing to scan.*

If you'd like to preserve the paper grain in your scan, use the Rubber Stamp to retouch the scan. I recommend using the pressure-sensitive Clone Stamp preset described in Chapter 13.

The retouched drawing

The drawing of the angel

Using Free Transform to scale the lilies

I drew the pen sketch of the lilies from life in my 9 x 12-inch sketchbook. After scanning the drawing into Photoshop at 300 pixels per inch at actual size in grayscale mode,* I retouched the scan using my stylus and the Clone Stamp Pressure preset described in Chapter 13. I wanted to preserve the paper texture (rather than clean up the drawing using the Eraser). Using the Clone Stamp Pressure, I retouched the handwriting from the lower portion of the sketch.

LEARN MORE ABOUT. . .

* Free Transform. . . page 93
* layers. . . page 34

Next, I opened the drawing of the artist at her easel (the working composite file) in Photoshop. I also opened the scanned drawing of the lilies and a third pen drawing of an angel that was drawn in Painter.

Choose the Move tool, and drag and drop each element into your working composite file. You can also copy and paste the elements into the working file. Take time to enjoy positioning elements in your composition.

2 **Transforming for more drama.** Take a good look at your composition. Will your composition have more impact if you transform one of the elements?

To create a surreal juxtaposition of elements, I increased the size of the lilies, making them larger in proportion to the artist.* I also made a duplicate of the lilies layer* and transformed this image to be small enough to fit onto the painting on the easel. I linked

Using a layer mask. For the utmost in flexibility, use a layer mask to hide a portion of a layer rather than removing the area using an Eraser, which is much more destructive. To add a layer mask to a layer in Photoshop, select the layer and then click the Add Layer Mask button on the Layers palette. A mask filled with white appears to the right of the layer thumbnail. To hide a portion of the layer, paint with black on the mask; to reveal, paint with white. Layer masks work in a similar way in Painter. For more information, see page 207 later in this chapter.

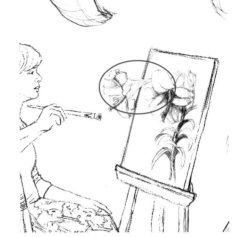

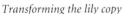
Transforming the lily copy

The small lilies shown using Multiply mode

The layer mask is in place on the easel

the artist and easel layers and merged them into one layer.

To transform an element that is on its own layer, select the layer in the Layers palette. Next, choose Edit > Free Transform, and while pressing the Shift key (to constrain the proportions if you'd like), drag on a corner handle to change the size. (I increased the size of the lilies by pulling on the handles.) When you've adjusted the Free Transform handles as you like them, double-click inside the marquee (or press the Return or Enter key) to accept the transform.

To make the white areas in the scanned sketch appear to be transparent, change the blend mode for this layer to Multiply in the Layers palette. I used this blend mode with the small lily and the lilies layers.

3 **Masking an element.** To make a portion of an element appear in front of another, you can hide part of the layer underneath using a layer mask.* So the lily would extend past the edge, I selected the artist at easel layer and added a layer mask. I painted

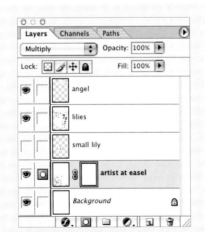
The Layers palette showing the artist at easel layer with its mask

on the mask with black to hide the portion of the easel. The effect can be seen in the illustration above.

Now you've completed the assembly of your sketch images. Save the file in Photoshop format. Then save a new copy of the working file in Photoshop format. To make it easier to work with the image in Painter on the next spread, merge all of your drawing layers into one layer.*

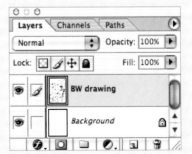
The Layers palette with the drawing layers merged

Adding Colored Brushwork in Painter

Broad Water Brush strokes

New Simple Water stroke

Soft Diffused Brush stroke with Pointed Wet Eraser and Round Water Blender strokes

ARTIST'S MATERIALS

Tablet: Medium-soft pressure

Program: Painter

Paper: French Watercolor Paper: a medium-grain texture

Paint: Mix color using the Mixer

Brushes:

- Broad Water Brush: opacity, grain, and blending vary with pressure

- New Simple Water: opacity and size vary with pressure

- Soft Diffused Brush: opacity, size, and grain vary with pressure

- Pointed Wet Eraser: opacity and size vary with pressure

- Round Water Blender: opacity, size, and grain vary with pressure

The composite drawing

Sampling color from the Mixer

1 Mixing colors. Experiment with color for your image by applying color to the Mixer. My illustration uses a palette of warm golds with accents of a varied orange, salmon, blue, and green.

The Mixer with colors

2 Applying colored washes. Open the composite sketch file you built in Photoshop, and add a new layer (in Gel mode) to hold the colored paint. In the Mixer palette, click on the Sample Color tool so that you can go to the Mixer and automatically pick up color with your brush

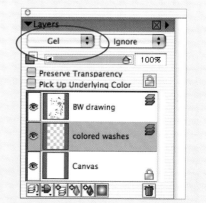

The Layers palette with the new colored washes layer in Gel mode

The short dabs of color on the clouds

In this detail, you can see the modulated color on the background behind the lily stem.

and stylus as you work. To add color in the order I did, begin with the background. I recommend using Digital Watercolor for the washes because this medium performs

A sensitive brush. The Broad Water Brush allows you to create beautiful transparent paint effects that are much like traditional watercolor. The opacity of the Broad Water Brush changes based on the pressure you apply, and the way it reacts to paper grain varies based on pressure. I love this brush because you can also control how it blends and bleeds into existing paint, by the pressure you apply to the stylus.

faster when you have a large file with several layers. (Experiment with the Watercolor brushes and Watercolor media layers also, because the Watercolor brushes can achieve richer texture.) To paint loose transparent washes, choose the Digital Watercolor category and the Broad Water Brush variant. For an interesting background, paint shorter brushstrokes of varied color to give the area an active but subtle modulated look. Use varied pressure and angle on the stylus for more varied, natural brushstrokes. You can see this brushwork in the large detail of the painting above. I applied washes of varied blues, purples, and greens to the background. Then I added warmer gold tones to the focal point area

(around the angel in the sky) and varied blue-green and light yellow-green washes to the foreground grass.

The background washes are nearly complete.

Adding light-colored washes to the lilies

Adding color to the stamens

The washes in-progress on the painting

3 Painting form with wet washes. If you want the foreground colors to mix with the background colors (as in traditional "wet-into-wet" watercolor), paint all of the colored elements on the same layer. If you don't want the colors to run into one another when you blend, paint the foreground elements on a new layer. I painted the foreground elements on their own layer, so I could control the washes and clean up the edges of elements with the Pointed Wet Eraser if needed. Because I wanted the colors to mix on the large flowers and the leaves and stem, I painted them on this same layer. Later, I planned to paint the artist, easel, and chair on this layer as well.

To paint form and detailed areas (the angel, artist, and flowers, for instance), you can reduce the size of the Broad Water Brush, or if you'd like crisper edges, try using the New Simple Water brush. To blend, experiment with the Round Water Blender.* I used the New Simple Water Brush to paint the central elements on the flowers. Then to soften the transitions in color on the petals, I used a low-opacity Round Water Blender.

LEARN MORE ABOUT. . .

* Round Water Blender. . . page 204
* Digital Watercolor. . . pages 108, 205
* watercolor. . . page 108
* preserving "wet paint". . . page 205

You can paint a darker colored wash, and then use a small Broad Water Brush to paint into the original wet Digital Watercolor paint with a lighter color and achieve subtle watery blends (as I did, for the angel).

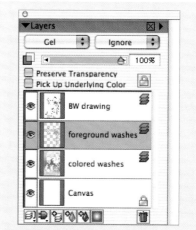

The Layers palette showing the foreground washes layer selected

Using a small Broad Water Brush to lay in the first color on the angel's robe

Going over the area with a lighter color, with a little more pressure to blend the shoulder

Adding touches of golden yellow to the shoulders with the small Broad Water Brush

Because I wanted to have control on the edges on the angel, I added a new layer for the angel's color. When laying in the lighter color to blend, use a light pressure on your stylus and dab the lighter color on. Then gently pull into the darker color with the brush.

For the angel's robe, I used a small Broad Water Brush to paint loose washes of blue-green on the robe, leaving white areas for the highlights. Then I chose a lighter version of the color and used more pressure to sculpt the folds in the clothing and to blend areas. To warm up the highlights, I added touches of golden yellow to the angel's shoulders and back.

Throughout the process of adding new layers for the washes, I kept the BW drawing layer on top. This allows you to add opaque paint on a lower layer if needed, while keeping the drawing intact on top.

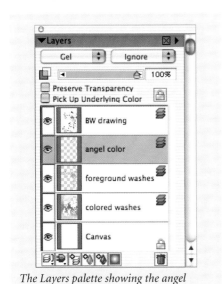

The Layers palette showing the angel color layer selected

Using a small New Simple Water brush to add color to the angel's flower wand, ribbon sash, and feet

The loose, light washes on the figure and the back of the chair on the foreground washes layer

Adding more vibrant color to the flower petals and stamen on the foreground washes layer

Painting loose brushwork on the stem and leaves on the foreground washes layer

Next, using a similar brushing technique that I used for the angel, I laid in light washes to suggest the forms in the artist's face and folds in the clothing. Because the artist is a secondary element in the composition, I used less saturated colors.

 A custom colorless Round Water Blender. If you'd like to use the Round Water Blender to blend without applying new color, open the Brush Creator > Stroke Designer (or the Brush Controls). In the Well section, reduce the Resat value of the Blender to 0%. Save your new variant for use later.

4 Adding details and texture. Now that you have the overall washes painted, it's a good time to step back and look at your composition. Are there areas that need more contrast? Would it help to subdue color in areas, or to add brighter color in an area? Where do you want to add more details?

For more flexibility, add a new layer for the details. To paint crisp-edged details, use a small New Simple Water brush (about 5 pixels).

Using a low-opacity New Simple Water brush, I painted darker tones on the easel where it was in shadow, and added deeper color to the interior of the large lilies. To make the foreground elements stand out more

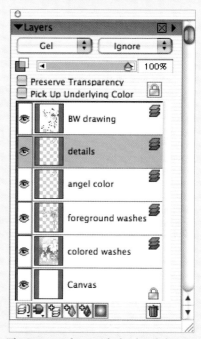

The Layers palette with the details layer selected

Adding vivid color to the small lilies

Using light pressure to apply medium-toned washes "wet-into-wet" on the clothing and chair

and the background have a subtle, rich texture, I used the default Broad Water Brush to modulate deeper blue and purple washes onto the background. You can see this color in the area behind the easel in the illustrations above. For the small lily growing out of the artist's canvas, I used more vibrant, saturated colors and applied them with the New Simple Water brush. To complete the artist, chair, and easel, I selected the foreground washes layer again and loosely applied medium-toned browns and blues, allowing the watery colors to overlay and to mix on the layer.

 Preserving "wet" paint. To keep the Digital Watercolor (or Watercolor layer) paint "wet," save your working file in RIFF format to preserve the native layer effects and Painter's native media. "Wet" paint allows fluid blending, similar to conventional watercolor paint.

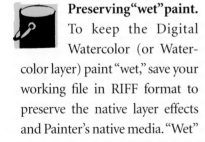 **Selectively softening and touching up.** In traditional watercolor, you can use pure water with a brush to soften an edge on existing paint. In Painter, try the Soft Diffused Brush variant of Digital Watercolor (sized to about 5–10 pixels) and choose white in the Colors palette. (White is analogous to clear water.) Gently brush the area with your stylus, pulling from the edge into the area of paint. To remove paint from an area, use the Wet Eraser or the Pointed Wet Eraser variant of Digital Watercolor. The Wet Erasers are also useful for brightening highlights.

The image before the lighting effect

The light effect applied to the filled layer

The light layer is now set to Multiply.

5 Adding to the mood. You can use the Apply Lighting effect to add mood and color to your image, to focus more attention on your center of interest, and to unify the composition. For the most flexibility, make a new layer to hold your light.

You'll need to fill the layer with a color for the lighting effect to work because the filter cannot operate on a layer without pixel information. (I filled my new layer with a rich golden color.) Now, choose Effects > Surface Control > Apply Lighting,

and choose the Splashy Colors light. This light has two light sources: gold and blue. The gold will warm the lower part of the image, and the blue will neutralize color in the upper area. For an effect like mine, make these changes: Click on the large circle on the gold light and drag it up toward the right corner, with the small end pointing up. Then click on the large circle on the blue light and drag it down toward the lower left. When you have your settings as you like them, save and name your custom light.

To blend the colors in the light layer with the image, change its Composite Method to Multiply in the Layers palette. I liked this effect, but I decided to keep the original clearer color in the focal point and

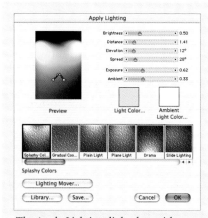

The Apply Lighting dialog box with settings for the Splashy Colors light

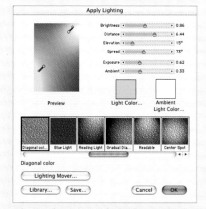

The Apply Lighting dialog box with settings for the custom light

Detail showing light around the angel

Enhancing Lighting Using a Gradient Layer Mask

You can create a layer mask in Painter, but I chose to use Photoshop for this layer mask because Photoshop allows more control if you want to use multiple gradients in a layer mask. I used the layer mask to hide areas of the light layer that I did not want to use.

around the artist, and use the light layer at full strength in other areas. A layer mask is the ideal way to (non-destructively) hide part of a layer that you don't want to use.

With the lighting on a layer you can control the strength of the light using both the opacity of the layer, and the area of the light using a layer mask. Building the layer mask is described in the following sidebar. Make sure to save your working Painter file in RIFF format. On a second copy of your file, drop the color paint layers to the canvas, leaving only the line drawing and the lighting layers above the canvas. To drop specific layers, Shift-select them and choose Drop from the Layers palette menu. Then save this copy in Photoshop format.

1 Opening the file in Photoshop. Open the image with the drawing and light layers, and colored brushwork on the canvas that you created in Painter and saved in Photoshop format. You will see the layers in the Layers palette in Photoshop.

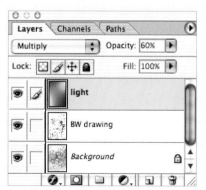

The Layers palette showing the light layer selected, with the Blend mode set to Multiply, and opacity lowered. The BW drawing layer is also set to Multiply.

The light areas that the mask will hide

2 Setting up for the layer mask. Decide what portion of your light layer you want to hide with the mask. I wanted to enhance the mood of my illustration by neutralizing colors in some areas, while highlighting the center of interest. To achieve this, I needed to make a layer mask with two gradient areas. This process requires a few steps because the Gradient tool overwrites itself if you try to apply it twice.

To add the layer mask, click the Add layer mask icon at the bottom of the Layers palette. An empty mask filled with white appears to the right of the layer thumbnail.

Return Photoshop's foreground and background color swatches to the default of black and white by pressing "D."

Pulling the gradient on the layer mask. You can see the lighter area created by the mask.

The first gradient applied to the layer mask as it is seen in the Channels palette

The selection loaded from the layer mask. You can also see the lighter area under the mask.

3 Applying the first gradient. To set up a layer mask like mine, choose the Gradient tool from the Toolbox, and in the Options Bar choose the Radial Gradient. (Again, set your Foreground color to black and your Background color to white in the Toolbox.) From the Gradient Picker, choose the Foreground to Background gradient. Position the tool and pull

Choosing the Radial gradient from the Options Bar. Select the Foreground to Background gradient.

the gradient out with the stylus. A long line creates a larger, more gradual gradient, and a short one creates a steeper, smaller gradient. To create the gradient at the top, I pulled about one-third of the way down the image, at an angle. You should have a white background in your mask, and a dark area where you added the gradient. This dark area hides part of the light layer. Apply the gradient carefully. It might take a few times to achieve the effect that you want. I wanted to create a soft glow, a lighter area around the angel that had no hard edges, so the soft gradient was the ideal tool to use.

By default, Photoshop overwrites the first gradient when you apply a second one. Here's a great workaround: You can load the layer mask as a selection by Ctrl/Cmd-clicking the layer mask thumbnail in the Layers palette. With this selection active, you can protect the original gradient and pull the second gradient in the lower part of the image.

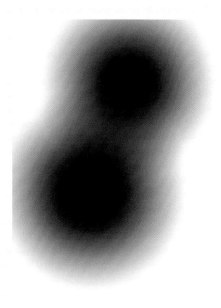

Pulling the second gradient across the artist and easel, with the selection active above

The two gradients in the layer mask, viewed in the Channels palette

You can see the soft light areas on the angel, artist, and easel.

Now that the selection is active, use the Gradient tool to pull the second gradient. If you don't get it the way you want it, choose Edit > Undo. If you continually reapply the second gradient, it can begin to erode the original one because of the soft-edged selection. The illustration above shows

my layer mask with the two gradients. In the illustration on the top right, you can see the two lighter glow areas that help to accentuate the center of interest. I was close to the effect that I wanted, but the image needed a little

more emphasis on the angel. To accomplish this, I painted on the layer mask right over the angel. In the next step, you'll brighten areas of your image even more by editing the layer mask using your stylus and a large, soft-edged brush.

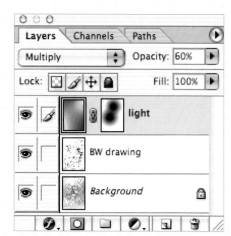

The light layer mask with its two gradients, as seen in the Layers palette

Editing the layer mask with a soft brush

The layer mask with brushwork, as seen in the Channels palette

Detail of the final image showing the enhanced lighting and final details

4 Painting on the layer mask. You can use a big soft brush and your stylus to paint on the layer mask and add to the gradient areas. I used this technique to hide areas of the light layer so that more of the original color on the angel and the clouds underneath would be revealed. I also used this technique in a more subtle way on the artist and easel.

Choose the Brush tool and the Soft Round 300 preset from the Brush Preset picker. Set the Opacity to about 30% and Flow to 50% in the Options Bar. Make sure black is still chosen for the Foreground Color, and that the layer mask thumbnail is still selected. Use a light touch on your stylus and brush onto the area of the light layer (mask) that you want to edit. For

larger areas, increase the size of the brush. (I used the brush up to a size of 960 pixels.)

It's helpful to view the illustration while you edit the mask. When you have the layer mask the way you want it, you might want to experiment by

The Layers palette showing the light layer mask with the brushwork selected

adjusting the opacity of the light layer. (I settled on 60%.)

Remember to save your working file in Photoshop format to preserve the layers.

If you want to take your image back into Painter to add more brushwork, Painter will open the Photoshop file and recognize the layer mask that you built in Photoshop.

I opened my file again in Painter and used the Runny Wash Bristle variant of Watercolor on a new Watercolor layer to add a few darker hues and more texture to the background behind the flower and figure.

Congratulations! You have completed the project. On the next page you'll find information about masked layer sets in Photoshop CS.

Masking using a nested layer set in Photoshop CS. The introduction of masked folders in Photoshop 7 allowed users to apply masks not only to layers, but also to layer sets. With the introduction of Photoshop CS, Adobe went one step further to allow the nesting of folders, each with its own mask. Although the steps I've outlined in this chapter work with each version of Photoshop that supports layer masking, current versions of the program allow far more editing flexibility. In this example, I began by applying a layer mask (the first gradient) to the light layer. Then I added a layer set (folder), put the light layer into the set, and assigned a mask to the set (the second gradient). Finally, I placed the layer set into a second layer set and added a mask to it. On this mask, I painted with the large soft brush. If I needed to edit one of the masks, I could do so without disturbing the other masks.

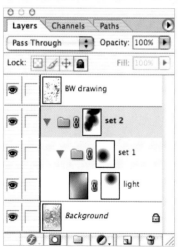

In this project, you learned about portability between Painter and Photoshop using your own drawings and sketches. You practiced sketching in Painter and then, in Photoshop, you incorporated scanned images with the Painter drawings to build a composite drawing. Next, you took the image back into Painter, where you added rich Digital Watercolor washes and a lighting effect on a layer. After saving a new copy of the file, you dropped the colored wash layers to the Canvas to get the image ready to open in Photoshop again, where you edited the lighting layer using layer masks. I enjoy this workflow because it demonstrates the strengths of both programs.

In the next several pages, you'll find a gallery of my favorite paintings that span nearly two decades of working with Painter, Photoshop, the pressure-sensitive tablet, and the predecessors of these tools. I hope you enjoy walking down this memory lane of digital painting with me.

Gallery

This gallery of digital paintings spans almost two decades of painting on the computer, and focuses on paintings that I've created for my own personal expression.

I painted the first black-and-white images using a mouse and Image Studio before I owned a color Macintosh and a pressure-sensitive tablet. (Image Studio is a grayscale program that was written by Mark Zimmer and Tom Hedges, who later created Painter.) Then, beginning with an early black-and-white painting, I created *Tranquil Beach, Color* using Photoshop 1.0. After this color image, I used Painter (or a combination of Painter and Photoshop) and a Wacom pressure-sensitive to create the later paintings.

Jake and Maria, *painted from the imagination using a mouse and Image Studio, 1987. This study demonstrates the use of early digital pencil and smudge tools.*

Wave, *painted from the imagination with a mouse using Image Studio, 1987. This painting demonstrates the use of early digital airbrush, and smudge tools.*

Tranquil Beach, Gray, *painted from the imagination using a mouse and Image Studio, 1988. This painting demonstrates the use of early digital pencil, airbrush, and smudge tools.*

Tranquil Beach, Color, *painted using a mouse and Photoshop 1.0, 1990. Beginning with the gray version, I created selections and channels in Photoshop 1.0 that would limit the paint. Then I set the brushes to use transparent paint modes that preserved the luminosity of the image. I used the Smudge tool to blend paint.*

Mesa San Carlos, *painted using a Wacom pressure-sensitive tablet and Painter 1, 1990. For this painting, I used a location drawing from my sketchbook for reference, while I used the Markers and Chalk brushes to lay in color. To blend areas, I used the Grainy Water.*

Coastal Meadow, *painted using a Wacom pressure-sensitive tablet and Painter 3, 1994. Using a plein-air drawing from my sketchbook for reference, I used the Chalk brushes to lay in color. To blend areas, I used the Grainy Water.*

A. Rafinelli Vineyard, *painted using a Wacom pressure-sensitive tablet, Painter 4 and Photoshop 3, 1995. This is an early example of mixed media on the computer. I chose a location drawing from my sketchbook to use as a reference. Using early oil paint brushes in Painter, I laid in color. To sculpt forms and blend areas, I used the Grainy Water. I used a hard round brush in Photoshop to add diagonal brushstrokes to the foreground and a grainy pencil in Painter to add more texture.*

The Alpspitz, *painted using a Wacom pressure-sensitive tablet and Photoshop 7, 2002. While in Garmisch, Germany, I painted directly on location using my PowerBook. Using custom brushes with captured tips, I first made a linear sketch of the peaks, then I added broader areas of color to the mountains, hills, and sky. I used the Smudge tool to sculpt forms and blend areas. To achieve a misty atmosphere in the foreground, I used soft-tipped low opacity brushes to paint transparent color tints.*

Agaves on the Edge, *painted using a Wacom pressure-sensitive tablet and Painter 5.5, 1998. While referring to studies made on location, I painted using several brushes, including oil brushes, the Artist Pastel Chalk, Square Chalk, and Grainy Water.*

Agave Meadow, *painted using a Wacom pressure-sensitive tablet and Painter 6.0, 1999. For this painting, I referred to drawings made on location. I also painted from my memory of the sparkling morning light and moisture in the air. To achieve a sense of atmosphere and sparkling light, I used a coarse canvas texture that would work well with the loose hatching strokes made with the Chalk and Pastel brushes.*

Blue Nude, *painted using a Wacom pressure-sensitive tablet and Painter 6.1, 2000. This study was painted from the imagination using the expressive Opaque Bristle and Round Camelhair brushes.*

View From Point Loma, *painted using a Wacom pressure-sensitive tablet and Painter 7.1, 2002. While referring to drawings made on location, I also painted from my memory of the sparkling morning light at dawn and the atmosphere across the bay. To apply paint, I used custom oil brushes and the Opaque Bristle and Round Camelhair brushes. To finish, I blended areas using the Grainy Water.*

In the Barrel, *painted using a Wacom pressure-sensitive tablet and Painter 8.0, 2003. While referring to drawings of waves and my memories of surfing, I used custom oil brushes and the Round Camelhair brush. To finish, I blended areas using the Grainy Water, and then added more brushstrokes using Impasto brushes, the Distorto Impasto, and the Thick Bristle.*

Agaves on the Edge, Summer, *painted using a Wacom pressure-sensitive tablet and the Artist Oils medium in Painter IX, 2004.*

Appendix A
Vendor Information

HARDWARE

Apple Computer, Inc.
800-767-2775
apple.com

Epson America / *Desktop color printers*
P.O. Box 2854
Torrance, CA 90509
800-289-3776 800-873-7766
epson.com

Hewlett-Packard / *Desktop color printers*
16399 West Bernardo Drive
San Diego, CA 92127
858-655-4100
hp.com

Wacom Technology Corporation
Intuos tablets, Cintiq, Graphire tablets
1311 SE Cardinal Court
Vancouver, WA 98683
800-922-6613
wacom.com

INKS AND SUBSTRATES

Digital Art Supplies / *Substrates
and Inks*
877-534-4278
858-273-2576 fax
digitalartsupplies.com

Epson / *Substrates and Inks*
epson.com

InkjetMall / *Substrates and Inks*
P.O. Box 335
148 Main Street
Bradford, VT 05033
inkjetmall.com

SOFTWARE

Adobe Systems / *Photoshop*
345 Park Avenue
San Jose, CA 95110
adobe.com

Corel / *Painter IX*
1600 Carling Avenue
Ottawa, ON
Canada K1Z 8R7
www.corel.com

Appendix B
Reference Materials

Here's a sampling of recommended references for both traditional and digital art forms.

ART BOOKS

Art Through the Ages
Fifth Edition
*Revised by Horst de la Croix
and Richard G. Tansey*
Harcourt, Brace and World, Inc.
New York, Chicago, San Francisco,
and Atlanta

The Art of Color
Johannes Itten
Van Nostrand Reinhold
New York

**Drawing Lessons
from the Great Masters**
Robert Beverly Hale
Watson-Guptill Publications
New York

Mainstreams of Modern Art
John Canaday
Holt, Reinhart and Winston
New York

The Natural Way to Draw
Kimon Nicolaïdes
Houghton Mifflin Company
Boston

COMPUTER IMAGERY BOOKS

Commercial Photoshop with Bert Monroy
Bert Monroy
New Riders
Berkeley, CA

Creative Thinking in Photoshop
A New Approach to Digital Art
Sharon Steuer
New Riders
Berkeley, CA

Digital Art Studio
Techniques for Combining Inkjet Printing and Traditional Artist's Materials
Karin Schminke, Dorothy Simpson Krause, Bonny Pierce Lhotka
Watson-Guptill Publications
New York

How to Wow!
Photoshop for Photographers
Jack Davis and Ben Wilmore
Peachpit Press
Berkeley, CA

Mastering Digital Printmaking
Harald Johnson
Muska and Lipman Publishing
Cincinnati, OHi

Photoshop Restoration and Retouching
Katrin Eismann and Doug Nelson
New Riders
Berkeley, CA

Photoshop Studio with Bert Monroy
Bert Monroy
New Riders
Berkeley, CA

The Painter 8 Wow! Book
Cher Threinen-Pendarvis
Peachpit Press
Berkeley, CA

The Painter IX Wow! Book
Cher Threinen-Pendarvis
Peachpit Press
Berkeley, CA

The Photoshop CS Wow! Book
Linnea Dayton and Jack Davis
Peachpit Press
Berkeley, CA

PUBLICATIONS

Communication Arts
Coyne & Blanchard, Inc.
410 Sherman Avenue
Palo Alto, CA 94306
commmarts.com

Design Graphics
Design Editorial Pty. Ltd.
11 School Road
Ferny Creek
Victoria 3786 Australia
designgraphics.com/au

EFX Art and Design
Roslagsgatan 11
S-113 55 Stockholm, Sweden
macartdesign.matchbox.se

Plein Air Magazine
224 Datura Street
Palm Beach, FL 33401
pleinairmagazine.com

Step Inside Design and **SBS Digital Design**
Step-by-Step Publishing
6000 Forest Park Drive
Peoria, IL 61614
dynamicgraphics.com

Appendix C
Fine Art Output Suppliers

My colleagues and I have worked with these bureaus that specialize in making large format prints for fine artists.

Cone Editions Press / *Fine Art Prints*
P.O. Box 51
17 Powder Spring Road
East Topsham, VT 05076
coneeditions.com

Digital Output Corp. / *Fine Art Prints*
2121 5th Avenue
San Diego, CA 92101
digitaloutput.com

High Resolution / *Fine Art Prints*
Camden, ME
207-236-3777

Nash Editions / *Fine Art Prints*
Manhattan Beach, CA
nasheditions.com

Salon Iris / *Fine Art Prints*
Vienna, Austria
salon-iris.com

Trillium Press / *Fine art prints; monotypes; silk screen*
91 Park Lane
Brisbane, CA 94005
trilliumpress.com

Urban Digital Color / *Fine art prints*
San Francisco, CA
urbandigitalcolor.com

Index

Q–R

S

![WACOM logo]

New! Wacom Intuos3

NEW! Patented Grip Pen

- 1,024 levels of pressure-sensitive control
- Cushioned grip for ergonomic comfort
- Three nib styles for a variety of "feels"

NEW! ExpressKeys™

- Strategically placed programmable ExpressKeys for convenience
- ExpressKeys are "chordable" and can be used for modifier keys and keyboard shortcuts

NEW! Touch Strip

- Finger-sensitive Touch Strip for quick scrolling, zooming, brush size control, and more

NEW! Five-button Mouse

- Patented cordless, battery-free, ball-free, and optics-free for smooth accurate tracking, reliability, and superior performance
- Ambidextrous low-profile design with a nice weight balance for just the right feel

Turn on the power of Corel® Painter™, and Adobe Photoshop with a Wacom Pen

The Wacom® Intuos®3 pen tablet makes it easy to quickly and professionally edit photos and create digital artwork by turning on the full power of Adobe® Photoshop® and over 100 other leading software applications. The Intuos3 tablet now puts ExpressKeys and a Touch Strip right at your fingertips for convenient keyboard shortcuts, scrolling, zooming, brush size control, and more. Intuos gives you control, comfort, and productivity.

Visit **www.wacom.com** today to discover the Wacom pen tablet that's right for you.